The Journey of a Hidden Princess | #TJOAHP

THE JOURNEY OF A HIDDEN PRINCESS:

A BRITISH LADY'S PATH TO DISCOVERY OF
HER AFRICAN ROYAL BLOODLINE

ANIKKA FORBES | Adepoju, Haastrup

AMAZON & GOODREADS REVIEWS

Lauryn

5.0 out of 5 stars **Speaking her truth.**
Reviewed in the United Kingdom on 22 January 2020
Verified Purchase
This book is about relationships and the extreme polarisation of the author's life. It shows how patterns created in childhood often repeat in adulthood. The book holds you in a seductive manner wanting more. The author holds you in a spell as she speaks her truth with no filter. The author describes a beautiful period when a damaged relationship with her grandmother is repaired. No words were used just forgiveness and understanding. A very interesting read.

Tanice Nedd-Smith **It Was Amazing**

All I can say is OMGGGG! It had me soooo hooked & I literally read it in 2 goes lol! It was such a good read, and it gave me an insight to what you had to go through which I think you were sooooo brave and you did so good with the cards you were dealt. Definitely keep writing & You've inspired me to write some poems about what I went through (I'd love if you could have a look at them whenever you're free if you like 😊. Thank you again for such a good book & I'm excited for any more books you may be writing for the future 🙌🤗♡

ACKNOWLEDGEMENT & THANK YOU

Firstly, the biggest thanks to the amazing, one and only almighty living god! Only he knows what is destined for us all and without believing, talking, or praying to him, you will never really know how wonderful he is all the time! It is my first book, and I am not looking for perfection (not that it exists anyway) but wow using this writing editor this year to do my final read-through and edits has made a massive difference. One thing I can guarantee is that it will be an interesting read and hopefully an inspirational one too. Amen

I want to dedicate this book to both grandparents on both sides, even more so to my Grandma and Nan, as without them, I would not have my parents. I love you both more than I ever got to show or tell you, so sorry none of my four Grandparents got to see or read this book, but I know you would all be proud and have read it already from up above I am sure! Love to you all and may you continue to watch over me. R.I.P. x

To my creator's aka parents, I hope reading this book (if you do) you can see the bigger picture of 'me' sharing some of my life stories. You might find parts hard to read and may even want to believe it is not true but God and all those that have passed over know, I have no reason to lie and if there is one thing you can both agree on is that **'I am too honest for my own good'.**

I would not change either of you the same way I would not change me because this is how God created us! Here you will both get to know some of what I have experienced in my life so far as a child through to adulthood and hopefully, it will give you an insight to me and my personality which I know you have found challenging at times. Though you are my parents; I do not think either of you knows me at all! For anything written that you may think I should have kept to myself, know that it is not about upsetting you or anyone merely sharing my truth. Love you both always and forever. x

Big kiss and thank you to my beautiful and talented Cuzie Princess Zehynarb, who was the person that made me feel and look like a princess on the cover of my book. Her hands done my headwrap and flawless makeup, too and I love you so much and cannot wait to see you, plus my precious Aunty Yetunde and the others again by God's Grace. Amen

Thank you to John Foscolos for editing the book cover and making it look so elegant and lovely.

To TD, still in shock to know that you are no longer here. Hope you are up in heaven continuing to do the one thing you loved riding your motorbike. You will always have a place in my heart. R.I.P. x

To my Agent, Jack Bypass thank you for welcoming me onto your books, for putting me forward for jobs, for your assistance when I needed it and though it was a shame we never met, I am grateful. Thank you for your time!

A big thank you to ex-reporter/writer Mitch my (1st attempt) editor for your honesty, encouragement and believing in me and my diaries. Then to Sabrina Guice, the fairy godmother (ghost writer, researcher, and editor) an even bigger thank you for putting the 'icing on the cake' when you spoke/interviewed my Dad! You suggested the Title then Book Cover and at that point, this was officially when my vision became a reality! Thank you again for your hard work, time, belief but most of all for helping to make my (want) from my teens finally come true.

To Max Maxwell and the lady (apologies), I could not find the details with your name! You both donated to my 'Just Giving' help request back in '2018 when I was on a low and needed more money to cover a few of the books editing cost. Much appreciated from the heart. x

Pastor Babatunde Adesilu I still cannot believe you to are no longer here, but I know that even from above you will remain to do superb things to keep all your family, friends, Dad and me safe and sound. It was not long, but I am so glad that Dad introduced us and thank you for your help and assistance over those three years of knowing you. Dad and I miss you lots.x

To Dee, the creator of the magnificent Body Changer, aka Body Messiah (blood and body) cleansing drink. Thank you for introducing me to your 1 in a million creation. It consists of two natural ingredients the **Neem Leaf and Bitterwood Bark**. I have felt and seen the change in my body since I started drinking it back in '2017. Honestly, it has helped cure people of sickness, pains, re-stored vision, weight loss and tackled the deadly 'C' to name a few, if you have tried everything no matter the problem once you start drinking this juice, you too will see the magic that it does for your body. Contact Dee via IG: **Bodymessiah**

I want to say a big thank you to Shah Nawaz for his professionalism, kindness, patience with doing the kindle formatting and for creating the Book Cover Spine and Back. I would recommend his service via Fiverr and he can be found under; **shah_nawaz17**

Thank you to those that know me on a personal level whether past or present family, friends, associated, work colleagues as I believe our paths were meant to cross for whatever reason. For all the jobs in the last 6yrs that I have done (contracting or entertainment) I would like to say thank you all for having me and grateful for all experiences. No regrets!

Last but not least a BIG Thank You, to YOU (**the reader**) for either being family, a friend, associate, a fan or naturally curious; whatever your reason for purchasing this book and wanting to read some of my life journey I am humbly grateful for the love and support.

If there is one thing that I can ask from you is to 'Believe in Yourself' and last but not least, please leave a review (good or bad) after you have read this book it would be much appreciated. Nuff Love to you all!

WOW I still cannot believe it, two-decades later I finally have something to be proud of and may the year 2020 onwards be full of surprising, unexpected opportunities and more. By God's Grace. Amen

'2020

TABLE OF CONTENTS

CHAPTER 1: WHERE AM I NOW... 9

CHAPTER 2: AKA (also-known-as) 23

CHAPTER 3: BORN OF ROYALTY 44

CHAPTER 4: LADY OF VARIETY 72

CHAPTER 5: NIECE, CRETE, ATTACK 125

CHAPTER 6: #TB 12 MONTHS 148

CHAPTER 7: SERTRALINE vs SEROTONIN..162

CHAPTER 8: UP, CLOSE & PERSONAL 172

CHAPTER 9: MAN, OVER CHILD 205

CHAPTER 10: 12.01.2012..227

CHAPTER 11: DIFFERENT FATHER, SAME   MOTHER 242

CHAPTER 12: #SWSWIB...252

CHAPTER 1: WHERE AM I NOW...

Well, firstly I would like to say I am now in November '2019 and the content of my book was written a few years ago, but it has been a challenging, stressful, and emotional process for me in completing this book.

The reason why I say this is because I have had to reflect on past experiences which I had locked away in my brain, so when thinking back over everything there were many times past feelings and emotions resurfaced, which did not make me feel good. It distracted my concentration and at times, stopped me from wanting to continue completing this book. But writing it out was simple, as I have always expressed myself in the exact same way that I speak and think, so that was fine, but the challenging part was the editing. The number of times I have had to go over each chapter to make sure it reads okay while adding, amending, and removing parts which I had overlapped on in other sections has been tiring, emotionally draining and boring at times!

I am sure there will still be a few typos missed, but hey, this book is not about perfection; only to share some of my life journeys. But I have not done this alone I have had the superb help and assistance from an American Editor/Ghost-writer who I found on 'People Per Hour' back in March '2017 and her name is Sabrina Guice of Lenox Avenue Publishing and Publicity.

Sabrina just got me, she has been like a fairy godmother and was passionate about helping me to make my first book a reality even more so when she (by chance) got to speak with my Dad, and he informed her about our Nigerian Royal Bloodline. It made her even more intrigued, plus, she is the fantastic creator behind the title of my book and suggested.

the perfect photo on the front cover. I cannot thank you enough, Sabrina, even though I am sure maybe she thought that this book would not be completed as it has taken two and a half years later. So, after receiving the final edits from Sabrina back in August/Sep '2017, I was excited and optimistic that I would have it complete and ready to publish by Christmas that year or latest by my birthday in January '2018. It did not happen, disappointed.com!

2018:
From February '2018 was my lowest state when it came to working having been unemployed for eleven months, not knowing whether I was coming or going, had no clue what work I wanted to do anymore. The final icing on the cake that is killing me till this day was the fallout with my sister-in-law which also took place in February where she decided to 'stick me where it hurts' by refusing and cutting all contact with my precious welsh babies (niece and nephew). Blocking me on all her social media, on the phone, even down to this year (Oct '2019) when I saw her details come up on Whatsapp a week before my nieces sixth birthday. I sent her a message asking if she could confirm that she is still at the same address so I could send a gift like (last year) though unsure if they received them. She had read my message and then blocked me again. Like, who does that!!!

I despise parents who use their children as weapons to hurt other family members; they are selfish, inconsiderate, wicked, and obviously, do not have their children's best interest at heart otherwise they would not stop them from being around those who love and adore them. It was me who drove three hours to wales to collect her and the four kids then three hours back to London all on the same day when I was so concerned for her safety due to her informing me about my brother being an arse and not staying away from the house. Her grievance is with me for telling her some <u>home truths</u> which had built up over the four years of knowing her; I have no regrets for expressing my concerns; sometimes **The Truth.**

Hurts and on this occasion, it obviously did which is why she took the last bit of family away from me!

If I had said to her what I did to be cruel and wicked, I would have written it here for you (the reader) to read! L, I know you are a great mum who adores your beautiful children, but I also know that you are loving keeping me away from my precious niece and nephew out of nothing more than spite! I do not expect her to understand the importance of them having some of their black family roots in their life, as two black mixed-race children growing up in the south of wales area where it is literally **'spot the black'**. People and children, in general, can be racist and cruel; so, she will <u>NEVER</u> understand how they will feel should they encounter any of this treatment growing up. No matter how much she believes that they do not need their other side of the family in their life, i.e. (me) as the only family member on my brothers' side who made time for them and miss them like crazy!

But who knows maybe within this year and a half she has built up a relationship with my mum and the others, maybe mums travelling up to wales to see them, or perhaps my brother and her are back together? If that is the case, I hope he is treating her right, the same way he would expect a man to treat his daughters with respect! #yerisaidit

On another deep note, again people do not think about these things, but I DO! Imagine, god forbid if either of my niece and nephew needed blood or a life-saving transplant and neither she nor her family members were a match, so they needed to test the black side of the family members. What do you think she would do? Do you think she would continue to 'cut off her nose', to spite her face' and leave her child sick or would she do everything in her power to get them well again by trying to get in contact, hmmm, answer that question?

The moment you become a parent, it is no longer about you but doing the best for your child/ren and making sure their safe and surrounded by

unconditional love and affection ideally from both sides of the family unless you have concerns for your child's safety or wellbeing. You do not need to be a parent to know this! But if I am honest, I should have known a day like this would come because whenever I asked her.

"When can I have them for a week or weekend."

She would purposely IGNORE my question, so what does that say; she did not trust me anyway! Like, what did you think I was going to do, never bring them back, dam joker!!! Yes, I am vexed, as I am sure you can tell because I have done nothing wrong to them and do not see why I must miss out of them growing up or their Birthdays and Christmases.

I can only hope it will not be forever! Anyway, moving on from that worst time during '2018 of possibly never seeing them again, things just continued to get from bad to worse. At least I can give thanks and will always appreciate my beautiful, yummy mummy Cuzie Claire for making me godmother to her adorable, sons (3Ts). I know I do not see them as often as I would like, but I love them all, will always be here no matter what. I am so proud of her she is truly blessed to have her soldiers for life along with the new addition. God Is Great.

I was no longer contracting on the fabulous £25m project, a six-storey mansion paying me £24phr. Then I had my car a Mercedes A-Class which I had for four years doing more sitting than driving along with car fines and a few other debts building up! Here are a few of my diary entries.

Thursday 18th Jan '2018: Yesterday, why did I have a Reinforcement Officer at the door asking if I am Anikka Forbes and as I looked out on to the road where my car was parked up why did I see for the second fucking time in about three-months a big stinking yellow triangle over the wheel. Clamped Biatch!!! WTF, no is all I could say to myself (out loud) Lol. He explained to me that it was a red route ticket, that was issued to me from six months ago from my old rental address around the corner, but I did not know. That is what happens when you move homes, too much. Kmt! (kiss my teet)!

Then when he told me it was going to cost just over £500 for him to unclamp my car, I nearly passed out! I had £700+ which was for my rent; I could not see my car taken away, so I need to figure out how to get the remaining money, yer right! The quickest option for me to make money quick would be for me to go and sell my body; even then, knowing my luck no one would want me. Lol! All jokes aside, not going to lie when times have been hard over the years and I have felt like there is no choice, this thought had crossed my mind, BUT it has never been that deep that I have allowed myself to go down that road no matter how many times I have thought about it. #justbeinghonest

Sunday 25th March '2018: I finally decided to sell my car (god is great) what a dam good thing I did! There were x2 Red Route lines added outside the driveway of the house that I am renting a room from, WTF! Considering I have been living at this address for a year now and this house the only one on the street that did not have those lines outside does now!

Was it because I disputed the ticket that was on my car a few weeks ago (fuming) because it had been parked directly outside the (non-Red Route) A40 driveway which I had been parking outside for nearly a year? Err, hello where the hell would I have parked my car please, had I not finally realised that it was becoming more of a burden now I was unemployed and in need of money to cover my rent for the next 2months at least! Even though there is a driveway, it is tight and not easy to drive into on the busy dual carriageway. I asked myself

> *"What is wrong with me, what am I doing wrong or am I a liability as to why no one wants to give me a great opportunity within this Entertainment Industry doing Acting, Presenting, Modelling or Reality TV". Kmt!*

I do not believe in limiting myself, but maybe I am trying to do too many different things; therefore, I should just focus on one and the others will follow! But I have been there and done that, how much can you keep trying yet feeling like you are never getting anywhere, and no amount of crying is going to help that's why I have not allowed myself to shed any tears! As low and rubbish as I feel I will not let myself break! FFS, surely it cannot all be me; I am not a terrible person! Yes, I can be a little clumsy, scatter-brained, loud, too outspoken, direct, serious-faced and certainly a hoarder, plus when it comes to my hygiene (keeping myself clean) it is standard procedure! Perfect does not fit into my category; I am simply #doingme 🙈

In my diaries, if I am angry, I will write about why and that usually helps me get through those emotions. My life has not been easy, nor would I change a thing because I know that I am a blessed lady because I have my health and ability. There are people all over the world who have been through or going through far worse, which is why I give thanks every day! Despite any disappointments from family, relationships or friendships, the let-downs that happen in everyday life, I know that no matter what, being an honest, kind, and thoughtful person takes you much further in life than being dishonest, selfish, and inconsiderate.

There were some fun times during this year, where I was seeing someone for about six months, I had seen him around a few times since living in West London and from the first time I saw him I was attracted to him. We ended up talking for the first time while at the Community Centre.

He was a great distraction from my dark times from the end of July till December as was I for him too as he had his personal stresses going on also! He spent days at a time with me, coming and going having given him an 'open pass' to visit and stay whenever. Great company and a regular enjoyable servicing at least three times a day plus he was F.A.W (fine as wine).

There were no complaints from me, though he had a lifestyle that is not for everyone, but it did not have any adverse impact on me, so no issue! One thing with me is I do not give my time nor get involved with any man unless I am really feeling them with the future potential of something serious, while there has been the odd occasion of liking someone but no interest other than occasional sex! But once I feel like it is the same routine with no change or unsure where I stand with that person I either let them know my thoughts, i.e., wants, or call it a day by locking-off any more personal time. I had given six months of my time in casualness, but I refused to enter a new year on the same flex because a relationship is what I require; **I want my one and only**.

So, I sent him a text explaining that I wanted to be exclusive (boyfriend/girlfriend) though his situation was not straight forward, I was patient and understanding, but wanted more which he could not give, so I decided to knock it on the head. The new year '2019 he visited me having brought him a little Christmas present (cufflinks) which he loved. Then in May he passed by and ended up having a final session and I closed that chapter. It was 'fun while it lasted'.

Cufflinks are a unique gift that only a handful of men have ever received from me; the first person given a pair was back in '2011. And the last man to acquire this gift was someone I met on a six-week course at the beginning of this year. I referred to him as Mr Obviously, he was down to earth, confident, charming, a great cook of 'jollof rice and fish' and most def give extra ratings to a man who cooks! He was into Entertainment the music side of things producing and had a few artists, I was impressed with what he was doing. But due to past hurt and betrayal which we had spoken about, I could see traits in him that I was not feeling, i.e., too jealous and a little possessive! Considering we were casually seeing each other and not exclusive, though still, it does not excuse getting upset or angry because I am speaking to other guys!

Any man that cannot handle a female innocently showing others a simple (what I call) **'Showing Luv with a Hug'** is a cause for concern; not to mention hating any I got whenever we were in training or working at events. It had only been the second week of the course that we had started 'seeing each other' and had already had a dispute! Do not get me wrong away from that all was fine! We enjoyed each other's company, he always dropped me home, chilling together, he stayed at mine and I at his too.

The chemistry plus sex was on-point (minus) his selfishness of always requesting 'oral' yet refusing to give it! <u>A man should respect a female if it is not her thing and visa-versa,</u> but occasionally she may give you a little treat, but if your adamant on **"I don't eat"** then you need to keep your skin quiet and STOP asking or go elsewhere! His insecurities that he was reflecting on me I knew it was going to be an issue. I expect a man to be proud and sure-of-himself when in my presence; even more, if you are the one, I am giving my time to (exclusive or not). I am not about causing any disrespect or making a man feel away, BUT unless I have given you a reason to doubt or not trust me, I expect you to see me speaking or giving someone a hug to say (hi or bye) as no threat! It is not everyone that gets a hug embrace from me, I am selective and all about aura, so if I don't hug you then it is because I do not feel that natural, real, and positive energy from you. #yerisaidit #keepingitreal

His birthday arrived, got him cufflinks with his business logo on it, they looked great and he was chuffed too when he saw them which warmed my heart. Anyway, minus the jealousy and the other #notimpressed.com ways about him it was a short two-month encounter and we drifted, but we have spoken a few times! Anyone that I have been **'Up, Close and Personal'** with there has never been any drama. Were grown and there are no hard feelings (well not on my side) anyway, Lol!

I am a person who will always touch base to see how they are doing. If I see them again while out, or they call to pass by or not, it is no problem! I do not believe you cannot continue a good friendship with someone you were once involved with regardless of how long it lasted as we all have a past and if you know, you are a trustworthy person then it is no biggie! It is the **secretive** shit from not being honest is where all problems start, but if you are straight up and have nothing to hide, then your mind is clear! One thing that I can always rely on when I am not sexually active is the DIY Power Shower.

The incredible **'clit'** stimulation for (females only) a guaranteed orgasm in a few seconds or minutes depending on the speed and how you manoeuvre your hand! I recommend you remove the showerhead, let the water flow out from the hose, then place your finger over the top a little, so it sprays out fast and hard; then OMG you will be in climax heaven! I prefer to stick with D.I.Y instead of continued sex with a man I am feeling and who is into me too but after a few months, realising we are not on the same page. So, I start to switch off and will no longer entertain or give any more valuable time; with no regrets as I believe they were only meant to be a part of my life for a moment!

HIGHLIGHTS OF THE LAST THREE YEARS

TV:
Friday 24th Feb '2017: I appeared on ITV's Judge Rinder. It is viewable via my YouTube Channel called **'The CHATBACK Show'** listed under the playlist called; ME | On TV

TRAINING:
Tuesday 12th March '2019: I started an SIA Security/Steward course which was presented to me by my helpful work coach Rene and had the training provided by a Security Company. Thank you, Tony, Jim, and Jamie, for the training you provided. Then by the 5th June, I received my SIA Security Badge then made a switch from DC (document

controller) to Security still within construction. The current project I am working on is the first job in my life where I am working 'nights' plus it is 15-20mins walk from where I live, a first time too! I needed a break from being in the office and this is only temporary until I decide what next, I want to do or try, but I enjoy DC work and will always be open to opportunities.

The hourly rates I received when contracting does not even come close to that as a Security person! But the truth is sometimes it is not about the money if you are fed up with doing the same job and want to try something new, you must accept that it may come with one or two disadvantages like less pay. #thatslife

DEBTS:
During October and November '2019, I managed to clear some debts from the last two years. Thank you, God. Amen – Then appeared on 'Judge Rinder' again for the second time this month (Nov '2019). I took my landlord to court (no drama) except for being in rent arrears so wanted to see if I could get it cleared before the new year and get my rent back up to scratch! It has not yet been aired but will be sure to add it to my new YouTube Channel where you can see the verdict. I am not yet debt-free as still have a more significant debt over my head which I am trying to pay off (sooner rather than later).

PODCAST:
Thursday 3rd October '2019: I finally created a Podcast via Anchor named; Diary of the L.O.V (Lady of Variety). It is in Audio format 'Keeping It Real' as always with plenty variety.

Sunday 24th November '2019: For a few years I have been thinking of possible business ideas but was not sure which to try, i.e., Accessories, Merchandise or T-Shirts etc. Then I started researching something that I could relate to as a way to see if there were other options (without) giving away too much. A smoothie, I know many are making them, but I have not seen any with this specific mix of fruit and veg which I have seen during my research. Today I made the concoction at home, brought it to work and gave my work colleague Eric a taste, we sampled it at the same time, and both LOVED it! Which is when he suggested I make it and sell it. I told him the ingredients, but I did not tell him the 'reason' why I used the specific elements and then created a business plan for the idea. So, going to make some samples and see what people think and take it from there!

"If you don't try, you won't know". 💯

Saturday 30th November '2019: I amended my Nicky IG account from (nickydaiaries_2009) to (ladyofvariety_diary) then finally to (nickyforbes_aka) in '2020. The posts consist of past South-East London photos, diaries to present dedicated to the Nicky side of me, Lol! Then transferred some of my past posts from my IG (anikkaforbes) . I want the Anikka Forbes used as a brand, business, influencer account by posting things involving creativity of things that I am doing, trying to do alongside my hobbies like Photography. To items I have purchased, i.e., Clothes, Underwear, Shoes, Food and Mascara etc.

PHOTOS:
The photos in my book are a variety from the '80s and from '2011 to present!

LIFE:
Apart from the above, all in general, has been great. I am blessed to wake up and see another day along with good health and ability over my 38yrs that I have been alive, which is the most significant highlight of them all.

Thank you again to you (the reader) in advance for purchasing and reading my first official Book. I hope it has you gripped, and you enjoy some chapters if not all! One Love to all. #LoveTheBlackness♥

Social Media: anikka forbes

Website: https://www.anikkaforbes.com

Podcast: https://anchor.fm/anikkaforbes

YouTube: https://www.youtube.com/anikkaforbes

Lotz Of Variety Online Store: https://www.lotzov.com

'2019

Sabrina Guice and Me in Atlanta '2017

CHAPTER 2: AKA (also-known-as)

For as long as I can remember, I have wanted to write a book. Though back in my teens, I did not know what it would be about, I just knew one day I would be a proud author. Believe it or not, I love to write and have been keeping a record of my life in the form of diaries/journals for the last 17 years, though my oldest diary goes back to (1993) but not much is written in it! Everyone has a story to tell, but not many would be willing to share theirs and for some that want to write usually only embark on writing the first chapter. So, after more than two decades of hoping to do so, I finally took it upon myself to begin my journey towards becoming a Published Author. For me, writing is therapeutic and allows me to express my thoughts the way some would find through professional therapy or counselling.

My diaries help me to release the feelings and emotions trapped in my heart and head. Yeah, I know what you may be thinking, why would anyone want to hear about my life? Well, I am certainly not saying I am better than anyone else, but I do think writing is part of my 'calling' in life and why I am open to sharing, like an 'Open Book' but private too (if that makes sense). I do hope that through this book, you *(the reader)* can relate to one of my chapters or be inspired in some way too by realising that,

> *"No matter what life brings your way if you can see the vision and where you want to be, along with drive, hard work and determination. Then there is nothing you cannot do! But most of all I say, If You Believe You Will Succeed."*

Plus keeping a positive outlook on things goes much further, instead of letting any negativity win. Though easier said than done at times, trust me, I know! Anyway, let me tell you a little bit about myself, Anikka is my birth name and my nickname is Nicky, given by family as a baby, I think, which is why I am known as both! I am a Capricorn lady who was born on Monday 12th January '1981 at Dulwich Hospital in South-East London. From the moment I was born, my life was marked to be a bit different than the average person, why, because of being registered at birth with the surname Johnson!

"What is wrong with that"

I hear you say! Neither parents' name begins with 'J' let alone Johnson. So, if you are confused, trust me, it has been something that has baffled me throughout my life and this fact about me hurts still till this day ☹. Do not get me wrong I know that we are all different, blessed, and unique in our own ways but here is a question for you,

"How many people do you know whose parents had a child and gave them a fake surname, marked for life on their birth certificate"?

Well, now, you do! My mother's surname is Forbes and my father's Adepoju, but they registered me as Johnson. Where they got the name *"Johnson"* from is a whole other story, which I am going to share in just a moment, though now as an adult I have forgiven my parents for this careless and disappointing error in my life. I suppose if you look at it in a positive, it makes me extra special. Lol! The Johnson child, who does not exist. I know people go through far worse that's life and like my Dad says,

"God does not make mistakes"

Amen, to that! It was legally changed to Forbes by my mum back in the late eighties or early nineties, which I have always used! The whole birth certificate situation was an indicator that my life would have more downs than ups. I would struggle to know who I am or where I fit in when it came to my family on both sides, which is difficult to explain but again it is what it is.

Did I ever feel like I was treated differently by any family members the answer is Yes, mainly by my Nan (mums' side) and a little by my Dad's sisters who I did not see much though I was their first niece! There was not that aunt and niece relationship like I had with my mums' sisters and I do not recall any of my aunties going out their way to see me, take me out or have me over to stay. Once or twice, I stayed over my Aunt G's during my early twenties, but as a child, I knew she was not very fond of me as she had always been the baby of the family until I came along! Though I am not making excuses for them, it would have been challenging as my mum moved homes a lot, where she moved, I moved too! #BlackGypsy

Communication back then was either house phones or the phone box. Mobile phones were not around until 1984 and only a few people had them, but the truth is you cannot have much of a strong bond or know a person if you are hardly in each other's life. As an adult now looking back on this, I can see those specific memories regarding my Nan (mums mum) was not of the norm! Nan's treatment towards me, I think is due to her own hard, sad, touching, tearful and unresolved issues from her childhood.

I am still evolving and healing from some of the emotional scars, which is known now as Mental, Physical, and Emotional abuse. My Nan did not like the fact that her daughter was pregnant, let alone by a Nigerian man (Dads' words) not mine! Dad grew up in Wandsworth, South-West London and Peckham, a highly respected person even now, who is not your everyday kind of man, which was an added extra that Nan did not like about him and he knew it!

I do have some good memories shared with Nan from my twenties, during her later years of life where she needed twenty-four-hour care living within a Nursing Home. On a few occasions, I wanted to have a conversation with her about the way she treated me when I was young by asking

"Why were you so unkind and cruel to me"

Would have been the main question. But could not bring myself to ask because never in a million years would I want to upset her with these bothersome questions though I could see the sadness and regret in her eyes as she stared at me. I would say,

"Nan, what ya thinking about"

She would respond with the same answer every time

"Nothing"

But I knew deep down there were things she wanted to say to me! Maybe she could not believe that I the same grandchild who she despised was the leading family member who devoted so much quality time to her. The regular visits, bringing her treats, taking her out for strolls in her wheelchair to making sure her carers' treated her right and looked after her well. Plus, finally getting to know the real person behind the no-longer cold, stern, solid barrier which she had up for years was no longer present. So instead of questioning Nan about those dark times regarding me.

I would ask her to talk about her childhood back in Jamaica by asking specific questions. Everything that I had been curious about while growing up like; her parents, children, and her life in general when she was younger. This was something never spoken about let alone mentioned, until now the twentieth century!

Mid '2011, I came across my birth-certificate while unpacking some items from my move from Catford in South-East London to Shepherds Bush in West London. It went missing years back, but I had a passport as identification, so I did not worry about the Birth Certificate. Though

I cannot remember why, there was a time I needed it for something in my mid-twenties, but it was lost therefore I had to pay for a copy from the Register Office in Peckham.

I received it, used it then put it away among my important papers and until that day it was the first time, I would come across it again, looking at it in (detail) with my adult eyes. Which is when I noticed that both parents' surnames were written as clear as day, whereas, in my younger years, all I saw was 'Johnson' and nothing else. Thirty years later, uncertainty and doubts started overflowing my brain but the main question I kept asking myself is *'are they, my biological parents'*. I recall querying about this surname at least twice with my mum in my younger years and got the same response.

"It was due to your Dad telling me his last name was Johnson"

Which is why it is on my birth certificate! Then I started thinking (how can this be true) when both had to sign their signatures to register me and it clearly shows Adepoju, not Johnson - why did they not give me Forbes my mums name instead, it makes no sense! Did the official naming part of my existence mean nothing to either of them! How would you feel if this happened to you?

Only my parents know the real reason as to why they allowed me their first and only child together to have a non-existent name without thinking about the impact, it might have on me throughout my life. As a spiritual person who is a believer of Angels, Spirits, Ancestors, Clairvoyants (Medium/Psychic) and have had my fair share of 'card readings.' They have helped me look at things on a deeper level through my twenties and thirties. But this time around, I felt the urge to go and enquire about the Johnson surname, so what would the cards have to say this time and would I learn anything new!

Saturday 18th April '2015, I had my first astrologist reading with a woman called Meera, whose details I came across in London's Metro

Newspaper. I was drawn to her ad straight away, not-to-mention feeling way overdue some spiritual guidance as it had been a few years (2012) since I had last had one done. It would be the first time of all my readings, where I would be asking questions about my parents, so when the time arrived for Meera to ask.

"Do you have any questions"

I replied.

"Are my parents my real parents"

And her exact words were.

"You were a mistake from up above and was not meant to be Born. They are your parents, but they're not."

How are you meant to process such words? Wow, now I was, even more, confused.com which left me unsure of what to think! I had my first 'tarot card reading' experience back in '2002/3 a recommendation by my friend Tasha and did not have far to travel being as I lived in Catford and she lived in Downham (15mins) up the road. Trisha is her name! Believe it or not, I visited Trisha nearly every year after my first reading, up until about 2008, for confirmation to certain things that I was anticipating and thinking. Having these readings was like the icing-on-the-cake I needed to understand and get my head around specific situations, instead of feeling like I was just paranoid.

Anyway, in 2008/9, I met another blessed spiritual person, named Angela aka Crystal, she is a Medium. We met through my Aunt M (work colleagues) back when our relationship was inseparable and always out together. Angela was more profound than Trisha. Her gifts allow her to communicate with spirits (those who have passed over to the next life) which is not a gift to be taken lightly and can be immensely powerful and draining for them too. So now I have a variety of three and would recommend them to anyone.

A Tarot, Medium and Astrologer reader, all have provided me with considerable insight over the years. They are all phenomenal women with their unique spiritual connections which run deep! Only those who believe and appreciate this type of service will be able to relate. I still could not help thinking after my reading with Meera that there was more, like a hidden secret, not revealed, regarding the Johnson Surname.

I would say during my mid primary school years onwards, at times I never felt like a wanted or loved child, but more of a burden mainly where my mum was concerned as the central parent I grew up with until the age of 19. Whereas my Dad, though mostly absent from my life, whenever I saw or spoke to him, he would always tell me how much he loved and missed me, so I felt loved though 'actions speak louder than words'. Seeing and spending time with him was the actions I required as a child; instead, it was years of rejection I felt from him and plenty of tears shed too! On the odd occasions that mum allowed Dad to have me for a few days, he would pick me up, spend time driving around, at his friends or his home.

But most times he would take me to visit my grandparents, then tell me his popping out and leave me there (to-go-bout his business) doing what young men in their early twenties did and more! As an adult, I understand he had grown-up responsibilities to do (or did he). Maybe I was a burden which he was happy to spend a little time with but did not know or have the fatherly maternal instinct to want to keep me with him for the entire duration.

I was meant to be with him and no one else! There was only me; no cousin's as I was the first grandchild, though sometimes I would go to play with my Aunt G's friends' kids otherwise I would have been BORED out of my head. Already, upset (though I would not show it) clock watching the hours going by, then fall asleep, wake up and most times he still would not be back to collect me. How else is a child aged between (4+) meant to comprehend this? For weeks/months/years on end, I would have been counting down the days till I next saw him again!

To then be disappointed and let-down by the fact that I would not be spending the father and daughter precious time together like I was made to believe. Had I told mum (not sure if I ever did) that majority of the time Dad was leaving me at his parents, may have been one of the reasons she was so reluctant at times to let me go with him. I do not know! But what I will say to all Fathers/Dads is.

***Do not let anything, or anyone come between you and your child/ren.
If it is meant to be quality time make it exactly that, all about you
and your creation because they are not children forever.
Those vital years you can never get back. What you show them
from the start impacts on them a hell of a lot when
they are given hardly or no time together.***

#QualityTimeWithDad

Then when it came to the 'let downs' by not keeping to his promises or unable to see me, for whatever reason. More feelings of rejection started to form, but also made me crave wanting to see him even more. I would cry so much; unable to understand why like my friends (at or outside) of school they had their Dads, but I did not have a regular Dad like them! One who made time for me, would take, and collect me from school, who loved me as I was his princess. Is this not the way little girls feel who are fortunate enough to have theirs in their life? Whether it be full-time or a few times a week - were naturally Daddy's girls! #YerIsSaidIt

My grandma (Dads' mum) was the complete reverse of my Nan (mums' mum) one billion per cent. Incredible, the love and affection that flowed out of her when she saw me (only a handful of times) that I can remember. The number of times did not matter to my little self; her greetings with a big and enchanting smile (something my Dad and I are blessed to share). I felt loved that is all that mattered, plus her big hugs and unlimited kisses too. It warms my heart and makes me smile till this day every time I think of my adorable grandma (one of a kind) who I miss so much and wish I had got to see her one last time before she died. Although I am sure, some of you may agree that half the time our parents are not 'appreciative of us', though I know there are no instructions on **how to be a parent** you learn as you go along but to love and care for your child should be the main two things every parent gives.

The reality is some parents do not know how to show love and affection, due to most likely not getting it themselves when they were growing up, so sometimes this leads them to make some bad decisions which can affect their child/ren throughout most or all their lives. Harsh words? Not really, as you will see as you read more of this book.

I know from the stories I have heard from other family members including my Dad; that his and my mum's life (where my Nan was concerned) was even worse when I was born and was a LIVING HELL for my parents. Eslyn H Duguid (Nan), was born on Tuesday 1st March '1927 back in Rock River, Clarendon in Jamaica to a Jewish father and West-Indian mother. Nans' father (my great-grandfather) was named Joseph Cedrick Alonzo Dupee; he was born on Thursday 14th March '1895, in Lucky Valley, Parish of Saint Catherine, Jamaica. He died on 27th November '1977 aged 82. His father was named Peter Herbert Dupee and Mother Mary Ann Coatsworth who was born in Middleton-in-Teesdale, County Durham, England, United Kingdom.

I found out this info from both my Cuzie Junior and his wife plus from looking on 'family tree' websites. It is incredible what you can discover about your family from these online sites. Mum back then was still living at home at my Nan's when I was born therefore mum had to abide by her rules, one of which was not allowing my Dad past the front door - so for him to see me (his child) mum would have to bring me to the front door out in the cold. On rare occasions where she was able to sneak him in by distracting my Nan while Dad crept up the stairs to her room on the fourth floor as quickly and quietly as he could, because boi, had he been caught they both knew she would get 'stinking mad' then curse bad words and chase him out! Nan felt no way in locking my mum out of the home when she was growing up. Whether this was the case when mum became a parent, I do not know, but I would like to think not! Yep, crazy but true!

I do not think Dad would ever forgive Nan for the way she treated him, which to some degree I more than understand. Thankfully irrespective of the risks mum took, she did manage to get Dad in the warmth to see me most times and for the times that were not possible bringing me to the front door was better than not seeing me at all! God did not play when he created me and mapped out my life; he made sure I was blessed with fight and survival the moment I was born. Which probably explains why the midwife who was delivering me ended up passing out! Lol!

This is something Dad shared with me back in '2015 while talking about the Peckham days and me as a child.

Fair-skinned and Caucasian people were Nans' preference she had time for them all day, every day. Neither did she hide the fact of disliking (her words, not mine) anyone **'too black'**. I can hear her saying it in my head, as I am writing this, which was installed by her fathers' abuse and dislike towards her and dark-skinned people though she too was Fair in complexion! But that was not the half of it; Nan was ruthless and that is putting it mildly. Only my older brother and I know the extent of the treatment I endured for years, in her care, whereas my brother was Nans' favorite, and everyone knew it! Nan had a severe vile mouth; I remember some of the names she called me like; **Ugly African Bitch, Black Bitch** and **Kong Teet** aka **Buck Teeth** after having my milk-teeth knocked out aged (6 or 7) in the playground while playing kiss-chase, Lmfao!

There were many other wicked, mentally abusing, and disturbing names, but for me, during my 'primary' school years it was standard to hear when it came to Nan, though very upsetting! I suppose on a positive note this experience has added to me becoming so thick-skinned in the world of everyday life; so not much surprises me. I have soldiered through anything negative that has come my way from my childhood, teens and to my continued adult years.

I was also deprived of food by Nan. For example, always giving me the smallest amount and my brother the most then refusing me anymore if I was still hungry. She would beat me if caught going into her fridge, freezer, or cupboards, to not allowing me to have any drink! Only tap water was I allowed which she had to give to me, but I hated drinking it. So, whenever she was not in there, I would sneak into the kitchen, run the tap then pour some water and quickly sprinkle some sugar (which was always on the table).

Then mix-it-up, to create <u>sugar and water</u> and drink it quick then rush back out! For the times that I heard her coming down the stairs (trying to sneak up on me) but her bones would 'click' so loud. SMH (shaking my head!)

That was my signal to quickly run and hide in the toilet (same level as the kitchen) then wait until the coast was clear without being caught (as you know) what would have happened a beating in my skin! At times she would be in her room on the second floor and the stairs (down) was opposite the kitchen, so if I were in the kitchen and she heard me, I would run again to hide. Sometimes she would purposely sit on the stairs outside the toilet waiting for me to come out and I would remain in there in darkness because she would shout if I turned on the light in Jamaican patwah,

"Tun ah fi mi light yuh nah pay nuh bill eena yah"!
"Turn of the light, you don't pay no bills in here"!

All this abuse instilled many anxious feelings in me which no child should have to endure, even now as a grown adult there are still traces of its effect installed in me when it comes to food. For those that know me will tell you <u>I love food</u> too much and can accept being called 'greedy' at times! I think due to being deprived; I can eat like it is going out of fashion!

Yes, I can laugh about it now because it is the past which happened so long ago, and I know my upbringing with Nan was no walk in the park and most definitely was not like what I saw on the TV!!! In all honesty, the beatings from her by her hand 'very rare'. Mainly a belt, the curtain rod or slipper/shoe (something I am sure many can relate too) was the norm, some may even say it is a typical black heritage way of discipline. But I never met anyone else whose Nan was like mine. It is not so easy for anyone to get away with child abuse nowadays due to Social Services!

Though some have fallen through the net resulting in death, at the hands of their parents; R.I.P. to those innocent children.

Nan went from an over-weight, super strong, cold, independent, hard woman who did everything for herself to a withering away, in both size and ability! To never again stepping foot on the ground to walk from the first moment she ended up in Dulwich hospital having been found by her son (uncle T) slumped on the bathroom toilet. It is bizarre that the same hospital I was born in is the same place where Nan lost all her independence, having been moved there from Kings College hospital before being re-housed in a Nursing Home where she received 24hr care.

In '2002, is when it happened, which resulted in her being in the hospital for a few weeks. Then she was diagnosed with diabetes and was not strong enough to walk so before I knew it, she was bed-bound. Everything happened too fast and before my eyes, I was witnessing a phrase that I heard many times, **Once an adult, Twice a child.**

This is precisely what I experienced with Nan. Wow, that is deep even if I do say so myself! Some might call it 'karma' for the way she treated me when I was younger, but I forgave her and got close during the last 10yrs of her life. Seeing firsthand through her smiles and eyes, that she grew to love and appreciate me finally and those bad parts of my life, were healed during her years spent in the nursing home.

I finally got to know the real woman who was calm, funny, humble, and sweet, which takes me back to an enjoyable memory shared with Nan, going to the Laundry. It was located at the end of the landing on the estate, I would sit for hours watching and listening to the therapeutic sound of the machines going round and round. Anyone who grew up on the 'North Peckham Estate,' will know what I am talking about and have memories too! They were giant big washing machines and dryers, so big you could climb inside. I think I tried to once, Lol! Going to the laundry meant waking up at 05:00 am, so I was half asleep when I had to get myself washed, dressed then walk less than 7mins up the landing with Nan.

Probably this relates to why I enjoy listening to 'white noise' playing in the background when I am either writing, laying down to sleep, in deep thought or chilling. A noise like; a dryer, a fan, rain, crackling fire, wind, and snowstorms are the main ones played on a regular. I also endured going shopping down the high street in Peckham and I hated it with a PASSION! I had to walk with Nan either gripping my wrist too dam tight or holding on to the big old skool, blue pram, with the giant wheels which she used to pack her shopping in (I can see it now) as if it were yesterday.

Nan felt no way to shout out my name and make me feel shame, in front of people when I tried to walk behind her as if I were some big person walking by myself on the street, too funny. Before I knew it, I would be right back beside her doing the **walk of shame** the typical youngsters view when out with their elders and could not wait to return home. Once back at nans and all the shopping had been unpacked and other chores done, I would get my time to go out and play on the landing or as I got older down to the Adventure Playground located behind the well-known Bradfield Boys Club. I was a real tomboy in my younger years so climbing, computers, marbles, Scalextric was more me than playing with dolls.

I wish Dad had seen her when she was still alive in the nursing home, believe it or not, Nan even asked after him on a few occasions, which also surprised me. The person that Dad knew during the seventies and eighties was not the same in the twentieth century!

If you knew her, you too would not believe that it was the same person who unleashed on others, all her past hurt and pain from her childhood back in Jamaica, by her father. The truth is a person is not born wicked, or with hate, it is what they have seen and learn, and it is a fact that

The first five years of a child's life are fundamentally critical.

The Johnson surname is still a sensitive topic for Dad to discuss because for him; it was the cruelty from Nan that caused him to feel ashamed of his African name. When asked about it now (2015/16), he said.

"If I could turn back the time, I would have boldly given my last name on your birth certificate."

Many years have passed, he realised and believes (as do I) that <u>God Does Not Make Mistakes</u>! He is the creator of life; we do not need to understand why he does anything because he the Almighty knows and that is all that matters! Dad says he could not be prouder and gets overwhelmed at times at how much we are alike — beaming with pride at having me as his daughter, his baby and princess regardless of the circumstances surrounding my coming into the world. I agree that the creator (God) knows all, sees all and so part of my destiny involved me having to deal with this in my life. Nan's love and hate relationship with Dad may have been because she knew he could not be controlled or manipulated.

He has never been your everyday 'Joe Public' (general public) kind of guy! But believe me when I tell you that the moment there was any trouble with anyone, including my aunt's boyfriends my Dad would be the first and only person my Nan would call to sort it out. As ironic as it may sound and although Nan did not like Dad, she also knew he was someone reliable and respected him for that. Though she would never say or show it! Sometimes the person you dislike is also the same person you rely on when you require help, or someone needs putting in their place. According to Dad, Nan disliked him because he was African although he had left Nigeria aged three and had been living here in London ever since. Dad is a British Citizen with his indefinite leave to remain here in the U.K.

The funny thing is to this day people never believe him when he tells them his African; they always assume he is Jamaican though we are all African descent! An original, South-London, old skool, cockney who is highly intelligent, streetwise, good looking, young at heart with a calm, relaxed and collective nature. Back then in '1981 the year I was born, Dad later had considered changing his surname 'Adepoju' to Johnson so that we would share the same name! Though he wanted to do this, it was too late because the Birth Certificate had officially been signed and registered.

My aunties and godmother always told me how much Dad loved, adored, and treasured my mum unconditionally so much that he kept her (high on a peddle stool) she had the gold, clothes, shoes etc. there was nothing my Dad would not do for mum. He worshipped the ground that she walked on and did not want her having any more stress or problems from Nan (her mum) this is an extreme prime example of what a person would do for love and their child.

But he realised that changing his surname was not the right thing to do. Thinking about what his parents' reaction would have been having gone through with it, would be like him saying he was (ashamed) of where he came from and his African roots. I can relate as it is how Nan made me feel for being half Nigerian to the point where I would never reveal it to anyone when I was younger. If they asked where my parents were from, I would say they were both Jamaican! I am not against a smack if your child is badly behaved (spitting, shouting, kicking, and slapping) their parent/guardian which I have seen so many times on the street and public transport. It is disgraceful, shameful and a big no, no. I think the saying **'respect your elders'** was lost during the nineties when teenagers were having kids as it was used by adults so much when I was growing up!

That saying will always count where I am concerned unless there is a good reason not too! I do not agree with the term **'children should be seen and not heard'**, but unfortunately many children are ignored or handled poorly so are victims of neglect and horrible treatments either in their homes or in-care without any hope of escape. Being beaten was standard procedure at my Nan's five-story home on Copner Way, North Peckham Estate and regardless of it all, I am alive and thankful every day. #ThankGod

I am sure some people will be able to relate to some of these treatments as I am not the only one who endure this during the eighties, seventies, sixties etc. Yes, this was/is quite common in black households, but typically not at the hands of grandparents (I do not think), which made the abuse I endured even more devastating. I would say it originates from the severe abuse black people suffered during slavery and colonisation by Europeans which were atrocious. Through personal growth and healing, I have learnt to forgive but will never forget. I know deep down Nan regretted the way she mistreated me! I am humbled; I got to see her sweet and enduring side. The bond that I shared with her during the last ten years of her life made up for all the years prior, though I will never understand how adults can oppress innocent children. None of her actions towards me was acceptable behavior and it must have been a generational thing because Nan and her friends would always say things like.

"Don't speak unless you're spoken to"

You would not think I was her grandchild! Which made me grow to be a rebellious, outspoken, and humorous child who started answering back whenever she'd anticipated for me to shut up, knowing it would make her even more annoyed, but by then I did not care! At times when I was sick and tired of her 'going on,' I would hide away in the living-room (3rd floor) which was always locked. Luckily, I knew where the key was so would quietly unlock the door, sneak in then close it behind me and sit in the corner (out of view). Or I would climb into the bathroom cupboard (which was warm and dark) until I was unable to fit anymore, Lol! When either of these two places was not accessible, I would go into Nans room, hide at the side of her bed under the window (right by the radiator) silently until I was too quiet for her liking, so she would start shouting.

"Nicky cum downstairs weh mi can si yuh"
"Nicky, come downstairs where I can see you"

Dad did not know the severity of Nan's treatment towards me, nor do I even think mum was aware of it and the impact upon my psyche and emotions as a child. Had I told him how she treated me whenever I stayed with her, maybe he would have dealt with her harshly! Dad did not joke! Although my treatment from Nan was disturbing, exposing the truth was never an option out of fear for the consequences. I did not want anything to happen to her. I think in most men, it is instinctive for them to be very protective of their daughters and female relatives. Although my Dad was hardly present in my life after he and my mum split when I was three, I have since built a remarkably close relationship with him since May '2015.

He is a permanent part of my life in these few years, has filled some void of not growing up with a regular father figure, which I craved every day as a child, through my teens and even as an adult. Thank you, god, for bringing us back together. I have cherished the quality time spent at weekends chilling, watching films, talking, laughing, and going out and about together. We have grown close now that I am an adult, we can talk about everything and reminiscing on the past when looking back on photos which bring back so many superb memories for him and me.

Our conversations now have no limits! Though he is my father, he is also my additional best friend and we are continuing to learn more about each other which is a dream come true. It is also amazing to see how much we are alike, and I love it! In our getting to know one another better, it is good to learn from his perspective his thoughts and feelings from the past, including the Johnson surname. Though I know (while getting to know my Nan) that she had some emotional issues that had nothing to do with me or my parents, though at the time it felt personal! It is true

"When people do not deal with their issues, they project it out on others".

They say that when you suffer from hardship, it means that you have a higher calling and purpose in life. The reconciling with my cherished Dad, happened at the right time in my life because <u>nothing happens before its time</u> it is all part of my destiny, which god maps out for us all before the creation of life! The cycle of coldness and name-calling was passed down from Nan to mum and I was its victim. I remember once in my teens while in a verbal argument with my mum, she said something to me, which I think is unforgiving, cruel and no mother should say to their child **ever**!

I am an adult and it still cuts me deep! Yes, we are only human, and I know we can all say hurtful things in the heat of a moment that we later regret and cannot take back and this is one of those. In anger, she yelled at me.

"I wish I had got rid of you when I had the chance".

Wow, Thanks, Mum! I would have been one of the aborted babies too, but God had other plans for me as to why I was born despite not wanting me! I love you mum always have though I do not agree with all your choices but would not change you for the world. I would be lying if I said I have forgiven those words said to me because I cannot as it replays even more in my head now that my relationship with my mum is non-existent!

A person who carried and delivered me into this world yet says something like that is a mother not 'worthy' of their child. Yes, I put it in the back of my mind and our mother and daughter relationship had its typical ups and downs, but I cannot forget because the 'mental scar' is there! I would like to think my Dad sees my drive, strength, and determination. Still, if I am honest, it will be through reading this book that they (both) will get to know, understand my ways, why I come across emotionless at times, withdrawn, sad and temperamental because life experiences have created me like a **switch.** I can be happy on a high one moment and quite feeling low the next. But at the same time, I know myself a lady not yet a woman (in my eyes) until I become a mother, god willing.

I am a kind, strong-minded, big-hearted, loyal, stubborn, and loving person with no 'filter' most times but has a clean heart and slowly but surely overcoming the years of feeling like damaged goods and unworthy.

All thanks to the guidance from Dad for seeing the ***'darkness in my eyes'*** and helping to bring them back to light. Dad has taught me so much about the past, including some of his upbringing and life in general, which has helped me understand him. He has made a great effort in letting me know about my incredible African Royal History, so regardless of the 'surname' there is no taking away the African roots that flow deep through me!

I AM NOT

EVERYONE'S CUP OF TEA

LIFE EXPERIENCES SHAPED ME

SURNAME RIGHT OR WRONG

I KNOW I AM A SPECIAL ONE!

Anikka Forbes

Cator Park Girl Secondary School

CHAPTER 3: BORN OF ROYALTY

Wow, wow, wow! Who would have believed that this day would have ever arrived certainly, not me! Both Dad and I at the airport together, Heathrow, to be exact waiting to board our flight to the motherland of Nigeria in Africa. It was a massive deal for us as our first father and daughter trip abroad and would be my official first-time plus Dads' first time returning in over 34yrs before I was even born. It was a journey spoken about a few times over the years, but for one reason or another, it never happened! Dad has always longed for me to go to the place where he was born and where our family ruled for centuries.

Mum was never keen on me going out there as she thought they might keep me and not let me return or worse; kidnap me instead! A few of my Nigerian male friends over the years had offered to take me with them. But I knew (for my first time) if I were ever to touch base and visit the land of my ancestors then it would only be with my Dad; otherwise, I was never going to go! If I am honest, I can tell you now that I never thought that this day would become a reality. It all happened so fast as we had only been reunited back together in May '2015, having not seen him since my (30th birthday party) back in '2011. Before that, it had been years of no communication due to being fed-up and upset with his continued absence from my life. Though now I am not living far from his home.

This holiday was mentioned by one of my aunties while at my granddads with Dad, a visit I have not done in years! They were discussing some of the family flying out to Nigeria in 2016 to celebrate Granddad turning 90, what a superb age to reach! I have never known a man like

Granddad; honestly, this man never ages, he looks the same from when I was in my younger years and as strong as an ox. Life has most certainly been kind to him. Dad asked me if I was going to go with him and the rest of the family on this memorable and essential celebration and I was like,

"Yeah, let's go and make it happen"!

I got the impression that the others in the room thought that Dad and I were *'all talk and no action.'* Maybe my Dad was thinking the same thing that I would not go, which for me was okay because I knew this was a significant holiday I was not going to miss! More so as this was a journey to Nigeria which Dad and I had spoken about a few times growing up, but it never happened so this time I knew we'd be going (no ifs or buts) as there was no way either of us would be missing granddads big 90th celebration. Honestly, I could not expect my father's family who barely know anything about me, to believe I was going to attend! So, it was to be an *'action speaks louder than words'* scenario. Looking back on it now, all I can say for anyone who thought that we were not going to be present on that fantastic journey, had undoubtedly been proved one million per cent wrong!

The months, weeks and days leading up to our flight date, Dad started feeling very anxious due to mixed emotions as he had not been back home since his mid/late-teens (a couple of years) before meeting mum. In the late seventies, my granddad sent him back to Nigeria during his mid-late teens (as parents of the African/Caribbean culture do) for either a more disciplined and stricter upbringing or to keep them safe and out of trouble till their older. Dad was not meant to return to London. Whether it was indefinitely, or until granddad had sent for him, we do not know. But he was not having non-of-it! He had returned to London from Nigeria, literally a year and a half later.

How he did it is a fascinating mystery story, which I am still waiting to finish hearing! Dad could not believe he was going back except this time; he was now a man and would not be returning alone but with his own (mini-me) myself his daughter right by his side. I, too, was anxious, unsure of what to expect and excited to be finally going plus meeting my other family members like my cousins that I had never met. I made sure to reassure Dad, as he did to me that all would be fine and was over the moon to be going together.

There is nothing I would not do for him; I love my Dad more than he could ever know. Officially it was going to be our first time away on any holiday together! But before I could get overly excited, there was one main thing that I had to get sorted, my Nigerian passport. So, when the day arrived for me to go for my appointment, I met up with my Dad, then we made our way to the High Commission of Nigeria in Westminster. I must say, I was far from impressed at the way this service was set up! The standing out in the cold waiting in the queue was a joke, so glad I had my Dad with me for company; otherwise, I would have been genuinely pissed-off standing alone.

Anyway, once finally inside, waiting to have my number called Dad and I are sat cracking joke then I hear my ticket-number called, so I make my way to the counter alone. There I am enquiring about getting a passport, which is when the man asked to see my Birth Certificate! FFS (for fu*k sake), who brought that please because I did not is what I thought in my head! I had to explain briefly the longness (situation) of not having my Dad's last name due to unusual circumstances regarding my birth certificate! Which is when he asked to see my mum's details and **AGAIN**, I had to explain that neither of my parent's surnames matches the one registered on my birth certificate.

Why could I see from the man's face reaction that what I just told him did not make sense and was all too much for him to understand or even register, welcome to my world! All jokes aside and to <u>cut a long story short</u> I was unable to get a Nigerian passport, so the only way I was flying out was by applying for a visa instead, which I managed to get after the second attempt. I required a letter of invitation from a family member in Nigeria, so I asked one of my cousins if they could write, sign, and email it over.

Then I printed it out ready for the second appointment. I will forever be grateful to my courageous, big-hearted, and beautiful aunt, who, for sure, is a 'woman in control.' Thank you aunty Yetunde. I had only met her twice when she came over to London to visit when I was younger.

A splitting image of my Grandma, she is the person who wrote the invitation letter for me and the rest is history! Nigeria, here I come, was all that was on my mind, but on the other hand, I was still in disbelief of it all happening, though we were just a few weeks away from flying out. The reality that I was going with my Dad having just had him return into my life full time, in less than a year was a dream finally coming true!

This holiday was (like no other) I had been on before, having literally only packed my suitcase a few hours before I had to leave for the airport. Why I do not know, it is like my brain would not acknowledge it until the day arrived! Late packing is how you forget the necessary things when you decide to pack/check your items lastminute.com.

I will not reveal now what I had forgotten, will share further on in this chapter what I forgot to pack! #JokeBusiness

Monday 21st March '2016, had finally arrived for our father and daughter journey of a lifetime. We were both ready and excited! Knowing none of it would have been possible without our great-living God bringing us back together. I cannot thank him enough because

Nothing Happens Before Gods Time

So, for anyone that does not believe in this saying should take my experience as a prime example! Anyway, we touched down safe and sound at Lagos 'Murtala Mohammed International Airport.' The first thing I noticed was all the armed guards in their smart and sharp uniforms observing, watching, admiring, and waiting to deal with any issues or drama, should it occur!

Some of them were watching my Dad and me 'hard' which we both noticed; I could not help but laugh (to myself), knowing they probably thought we were a couple! There is no way they would believe he was my Dad or me, his daughter, so we were waiting for one of them to approach or say something, while at the same time I was thinking (please let this process through the airport) be a smooth one! Well, Dad, my aunt plus her partner who we travelled with all went through ok, then when it came to my passport, I was told to wait to one-side while the officer went to check whatever they needed to check. Straight away I thought

'hello, where are they trying to go with my passport'?

So, I followed behind him, keeping a close eye on it. Dad could see what was going on, so came over to find out what the hold-up was, then they asked who he was, and he responded

"I am her father."

Their eyes widened in surprise, one of the officers looked like he was nearly going to pass-out, LMFAO! You see, although my Dad is in his late fifties, youthfulness is on his side and he has always carried himself well compared to some men within that age group. He does not look his age, instead ten-fifteen years younger and as the true saying goes.

"Black Don't Crack… Unless You're Taking It"

Once finally out of the airport we took a cab to the hotel in Lagos. Here is where we would all be staying for a few days until we found another accommodation, where we could all stay together under one roof. My grandparent's family home is in Ilesha, not Lagos, which is a three/four hour-drive between both, so due to the distance, the big 90th was being held in Lagos instead. Granddad is a calm, cool and collective man who does not say much but is very observant. I am sure Dad, and I made the birthday celebration even more special due to us both being his firstborn son and grandchild to join him in Nigeria. I think he may have been a little overwhelmed at first when he saw both Dad and I arrive at the hotel.

As I am sure even granddad never expected either of us to make it, but we did! I felt proud of both Dad and me for finally making the journey that I thought would never happen. One thing about Nigerians is that when we celebrate something, we do it to the fullest. From fresh new handmade outfits (designed to specific colours galore and designs) along with so much splendor and much more! Everyone who had not seen my Dad in all those years was so excited and overwhelmed they honestly could not get enough of him. For those that he met for the first time were even more delighted to be introduced to him. Then when he introduced me, none of them could believe I was his child nor how much they thought I resembled my grandma. I was as excited to meet them as they were in meeting me.

As the days passed, we were either strolling around or out and about. Whenever we were speaking to people, they kept assuming I was my Dad's wife or him, my husband, Lol! Dad could not get his head around how much attention was being drawn to us or people's assumptions. For me, it is #standardprocedue hearing lovely compliments from people about either of my parents looking splendid for their age.

For Dad, it was all new and he loved it! It certainly made him feel even more proud of being my father. I have always had a yummy Daddy who, in a few old photos, looks like the good-looking American singer-songwriter Keith Sweat whose songs I use to play continuously in the nineties. I mean, who does not love his music or his looks. I certainly do!

Back in '2017, when I was working on The Scalpel project in Bank when one of my work colleagues thought the photo on my desk of my Dad and me was the splendid, handsome and talented actor Denzel Washington. Wow, that is a first I had ever heard someone say that and most def an absolute honour for them to think my Dad looked like him! My colleagues surprised face when I told him the man was my father; it is a reaction I will not forget in a hurry and a charming compliment made about my Dad.

The same goes for my beautiful mum as it is like the older, she gets; age does not catch up with her; another one blessed with youthfulness too. Flawless skin and youthful looks run on both sides of the family; people often think I am younger than what I am, which also depends on how I have my hair styled. I always said to myself (from a young age) if I ever changed my hair then it would only be into locs, which was inspired by a close, family friend who I grew up around and referred to as a cousin.

The one-and-only beautiful and talented singer-songwriter Caron Wheeler from the group Soul2Soul who sung (Back to Life). I loved everything about her sophisticated, long, flowing Locs and her voice and it was in April '2017 when I had my hair interlocked into Locs, plus added hair to the ends for length down to my bum and love the change. I cannot express enough how happy I am to have Dad back in my life in so many ways, it is unreal. Although he has not been present for most of my life, I have still always seen him as a protector, friend, advisor and just a straight-up gent who is loved by many.

I have two old-school friends who sadly did not get the chance to meet, see or grow with their fathers due to dying when they were babies. Chanel (one of the two) and my close friend still till this day, lost her father in one of London's historical disasters; **'The Newcross Fire'**, which happened six-days after I was born. R.I.P to Peter Campbell (Chan's Dad) and the 12 who lost their lives that night in the tragic fire.

On the positive side, both friends have exceptional mothers. Their mums' have always shown and given them unconditional love and support while doing the role of both mum and Dad, which I admire tremendously. They are both so fortunate to have the solid relationships with their mothers that they do!

While in Nigeria, I got to meet so many new family members, but only one stood out among them all. We were inseparable and instantly drawn to one-another as if we had known each other for years. This young lady is my beautiful, talented, funny, and precious cousin Zehynarb, who is a superb make-up artist. Granddad's birthday celebration was a splendid one, where for the first time I got to wear a traditional handmade full African outfit and felt like a trillion dollars. There was only one part of my granddads' party that I was far from impressed with due to us (family) turning up to the hall with not one table or chair available for any of us to sit down! The place was packed; there was at least half of the guest that was unknown to my granddad.

They had no shame whether they knew the person only that it was a party with free food, drink, and music. In my opinion, no one should have been allowed to enter the hall until we (the leading party) had arrived and been seated at our tables. This is how it should have been arranged, out of respect for granddad on his big day. It was indeed something to behold! Apart from that, all went well! Remember when I had mentioned earlier that I would let you know what it was that I had forgotten to pack for the trip, can you guess what it was? Keeping in mind my time in Nigeria was for (three and a half weeks) and what I forgot was ESSENTIAL for the trip but not the end of the world! As I started unpacking my bag, I realised that the only pair of knickers and bra I had were the ones I was wearing, SMH (shaking my head)!

I could not fucking believe it, **never** had anything like this happen to me before! My fresh new Primarni (Primark) underwear was back home in London. The brain was so excited and overwhelmed by everything (travelling to Nigeria) and rushing while packing. I suppose I was bound to leave something behind but did not expect it to be my underwear!!!

I was so disappointed with myself. But I am 'keeping it real' as this is what happened. Simple! Another person may not have included this in their book as I have, but I have nothing to hide because I am too **honest-for-my-own-good** and still cannot believe it, even now. I am a clean and hygienic lady so feel no shame to share this with you. Whereas someone else may have worn the same pair of underwear every day and night without even washing them, not me mate! One thing I learned from a young age from Nan (mums, mum) was to be extra clean 'as a girl child' and make sure my surroundings are tidy. I respect my body as though it was a temple (except when it comes to food) Lol, working progress!

Anyway, I made sure I washed my underwear each night, guaranteed it would be dry by the next day due to the superb hot weather ready to wear the following day. Occasionally I did not wear any because there is nothing wrong with going commando! I fell in love with the weather in Nigeria because I am a HEAT fanatic, so much so that I even brought my fan-heater in my suitcase just in case the air-con was too cold for me during the night. Yet, I forgot my underwear, who does that please, hands up, only me!!!

England, UK is a very damp, depressing, cold and temperamental country when it comes to its weather, even during the spring and so-called summer seasons. If we had balanced weather with a guaranteed hot summer season, then it would be perfect! Anyway, while I was lapping up the gorgeous African weather, Dad had me in Nuff stitches laughing, due to him not having the sun in his skin like this in decades! He hid anywhere with shade and kept complaining about the heat to one point I told him to

"Embrace it and stop moaning"

Lmfao! I more than understand it was a lot for him to adjust to coming from England as he had never travelled anywhere except now (returning home) forty-plus years later. Whereas me, I would rather have the heat any day over any dead, cold, and unpredictable London weather. African food am I a lover of it! I can confess (not really) as some might expect. My time out in Nigeria saw me eat only Jollof Rice (love it) Fish and Puff-Puff (dumplings). It is my Jamaican roots (mother's side) that I grew up eating and cannot get enough of it! For me, there is no comparison when it comes to both!

There is nothing that I do not eat I love cornmeal porridge, oxtail, curry-goat, rice, and peas, ackee and saltfish, patties, festival, rum punch, and the variety of soups and more. What is there not to LOVE!!! You name it; I eat it without any complaints! I love my food including Chinese, Italian, Persian, Indian, Mexican, and American, to name a few. In Nigeria, eating is incredibly special and intimate. When you join others for a good meal, it is the time for bonding in African culture, not just feeding your hunger. I think that is something you see in a few cultures around the world. Whether on the continent of Africa, the Caribbean or somewhere in the diaspora black people we love to enjoy a delicious, well-seasoned, tasty, and well-cooked meal.

It is all about enjoyment, eating and drinking. Before I realised it, the time had come for me to return to Britain. The day arrived three and a half weeks later for me to fly home alone due to Dad staying on for another, two-weeks along with granddad and one of my aunts'. They, too, were also staying a little longer. I was not ready to leave just yet! Especially as a few days before departing, I was supposed to travel with them to our family home in Ilesha.

It was the (central part) of the trip that I wanted to see with Dad. But my aunt, for some reason, changed the plans last minute! Deciding that they (Dad, granddad, and her) would go after I had flown back home! I could not understand why the sudden change, I felt very dishearten and segregated (nothing new). Even my Dad could not understand it, but we both said nothing more about it! Had I not needed to get back to London because of work; though I was fortunate enough to be able to work while abroad, otherwise, I would have extended my flight for another week so that I could have made the added much-wanted journey to Ilesha where my beautiful grandma is (laid to rest) within the grounds of the family home. I looked at the bigger picture by putting my feelings aside and focusing on my Dad as this added trip was all about him (in my eyes) finally getting to see his mother's resting place for the first time and pay his respects 19yrs later.

He got the chance to see, speak and spend quality time with his queen, his everything who he would have exchanged places within a heartbeat if it meant grandma would still be alive. Dad did not get to fly out and attend her funeral, due to her death crippling his mind, body, and soul 😔 for a long, long while after she passed. I thank God for my wonderful step-mum for always being there for my Dad, building him back up even more so during this tragic time though I wish I had been there too as support! It cuts Dad (till this day) very deep for not attending the funeral. A loss of a mother is a pain that I am sure never disappears, depending on the child/parent relationship!

Even if you have a strained relationship with your mum, the fact is, she is still your mother and the woman that gave birth to you!

Princess Elizabeth Adebimpe Adepoju (nee Haastrup) was the name of my grandma. A princess, WOW, never in a million years would I have believed I would find out in my mid-thirties that she was a princess, and my roots are of an African Royal-Bloodline. Only god knows how extra blessed I feel to have known, spent time, been hugged, and loved so much by my beloved Grandma, though I only remember seeing her a few times at the family home. I remember her big radiant smile, which is a replica of both Dad and I when we smile, you cannot miss our pearly-white teeth and gums! Her unconditional love and affection towards me without a 'shadow of a doubt' let me know that Grandma loved and adored me, the same way I loved and adored her too. x

It breaks my heart that none of the family told me all those years ago, that my grandma was sick and dying from that devil sickness beginning with the letter '**C**'. I hate the word so much; I refuse to mention its name because it is not (worthy) that is how much I despise it!!! Dad should have been the one who broke the news about Nans' sickness, but I would say he was in disbelief of it all. To hear that his gem-of-a-mother was ill would have felt like a bad dream! Grandma died back in 1997, which is when Dad (I think) encountered his darkest, most depressed plus vulnerable time ever. A broken man, like a child who could do nothing but cry day and night. My step-mum explained he was so bad that she had to give him something which helped prevent him from crying. His emotions would feel like it, but no more tears would fall!

All because of her fantastic quick-thinking and caring nature, she helped restore him to his usual self. I wish I had been there as support; though it would have crushed me to witness him in that state! So sorry I was not there for you, Dad. At the same time, how could I have been when only 16 and none-the-wiser! If grandma were here with me right now, I would tell her how much I love her, how much she means to both Dad and me including last but not least a huge THANK YOU for leaving me her precious, stunning, personalised necklace and earrings. Her gift was handed to me by Dad a few months after our reuniting back in '2015.

I wish I could have given her an everlasting, long hug to let her know my gratitude for receiving such a priceless gift, which I will cherish forever.

As I am writing these words, it scares the living daylight out of me because I have always (for as long as I can remember) suffered from cramps and pains in my stomach for years, but this I think is down to my gluten intolerance which I learnt about a few years ago. Either way, I pray to God each day to please keep me healthy and safe as I would not wish any sickness, suffering, let alone the deadly 'C' the six-letter word that I hate but so happy for all who have survived it. There are no illnesses in the world that are good!

I wish anyone that is currently unwell or who has overcome a sickness to stay strong be positive and believe that you will get better, as none of us knows what we are meant to experience in our life on this earth nor when or how we will die. All we can do is try to live the best we can, eat healthy with natural foods, remedies plus keep your brain active and exercise more because we only have one body in this lifetime and like Jim Rohn said.

'Take Care of Your Body. It's the Only Place You Have to Live'.

If you are reading this book while battling a sickness, I also encourage you to write whenever you can about your personal experience through the process. So that when you come out on the other side fit and well, you will have your own real and raw material in writing to look back on and who knows you may want to share it with the world by writing a book, which will more than likely help others. I know you will be so proud of yourself. We all have a story to tell, no matter where you are in life! #RealTalk

As a child of an African immigrant, this trip to Nigeria reconnected me to my roots. It helped to confirm in me that I come from a proud and regal people. To have been in Nigeria around my added family was a spiritual connection for me. It was a way to connect with a part of me I never knew existed, though there is still so much to learn and see out there. People from all over the world are familiar with the African proverb that says,

"It Takes A Village to Raise A Child"

Africans understand the power of communal living. We are people who love family and friends. Have always taken pride in the birth of a child as they are the key to the future of Africa and the continuance of our family lineage. Children are highly regarded in Africa. Are the Africans more equipped to raise children than in other places? No, most certainly not, but Africans are the oldest people of the world that birthed and raised children, so their voice should be heard! Africans carry the world's first history of building a society through the reproduction of children. Nations come out of children who grow up to be adults.

With more Africans migrating west for economic and educational advantages, more children of these immigrants will be born in the west. These children will be raised by African parents who hold the traditional values in a western world that seems at times to be on the opposite of their experience.

These children will be projecting an image to the world. Will that image be more western than African, or will there be a balanced blend of both seen in them? African parents will be facing a dilemma in raising children who also are competing for their place within pop culture, music, social media, and all other things that direct the attention of western youth. Whether these parents realise it or not, they are in a unique position in shaping the future of some potentially influential leaders.

After my Dad returned from Nigeria, he informed me about our Royal Nigerian Bloodline, along with three amazing and historic photos of his grandfather, who was a king in Nigeria. My great-grandfather's name was **Oba Alexander Adejumola Haastrup'.** I googled to find out more about this extraordinary family history and both Wikipedia and Nigerian Wiki have exceptional information. What you are about to read has been copied and pasted from the Nigerian Wiki.

Fredrick Kumokun Adedeji Haastrup *was born ca 1820, he was born into the family of a member of the* ***ancient Oro [Oro, so gudu gudu]***

Royal house of Ilesha. *It is one of the four ruling families in Ilesa and has been since the reign of Owa Obokun Atakumosa 900 years ago, whose four sons rotated the throne. Following Kumokun's illustrious reign, the 'Oro' family has subsequently adopted the Haastrup name. Around 1824, while on an errand, Haastrup was kidnapped and subsequently sold as a slave, he was transferred from one market to the other for about five months before reaching the coast where he boarded a slave ship with chains around his neck and tied to other slaves.*

Though the ship had a British Union Jack; it was actually a Danish vessel. At sea, Kumokun became frail, on noticing the weariness of Kumokun, the captain, a Danish named Haastrup released Kumokun of the chains and took care of the sickly boy. While on sea, Britain abolished slavery and the vessel subsequently lost its legal cover. The slave vessel was later intercepted by British Man-O-War marines and the slaves were diverted to Sierra Leone. In Sierra Leone, Haastrup became a ward of capt Haastrup who sponsored his education, ultimately leading to a license in town planning. Haastrup later decided to reunite with his old country, [Ijesha | Ijeshaland] and returned to Lagos, **by 1860, he had re-acquainted himself with Ijesha royalty**.

In Lagos, he acquired large tracts of property at Ibeju Lekki and present-day Igbobi, which he used to plant Kola-nut. Hence, it became known as igbo-obi Haastrup, subsequently shortened to Igbobi. Haastrup became known in Ijesaland during the Kiriji war [1877-1893] when as a member of the Ekiti parapo solidarity group in Lagos, the society supplied arms to Ijesha warriors who were fighting Ibadan at the time. He later was a pivotal man as an adviser to the Owa in peace negotiations with the British and Ibadan that ended the war. In 1896, he was invited to become the Owa Obokun of Ijeshaland. He is credited with introducing Methodism to Ijeshaland in 1896.

All this has the (wow factor) written all over it. So compelling that it makes me feel even more proud of his life struggle, survival, and accomplishments. Between Grandmas **Haastrup** and Granddads **Adepoju** names, they are two African surnames with a lot of meaning and history behind both. Adepoju is a surname of Yoruba origin, meaning **'the King/Crown/Royalty became plenty.'** People with this surname include Mutiu Adepoju (born 1970), Nigerian footballer. Sikiru Adepoju (born 1950), Nigerian drummer.

From the day I was born, my Dad has always called me 'princess.' I am the firstborn out of sixteen grandchildren and my Dad is the first son of his six sisters and one brother, which in my eyes makes us extra special as we are both first-borns in our family tree. When I found out that my grandma was a princess and that her father was a king, it was all so surreal simply because the only royal family we hear about is the British Monarchy. Now I know that unlike many fathers who also call their daughters 'Princess' there was always a real meaning behind why Dad called me it because I am a descendant of royalty! I think there is something to be said of bloodline.

I believe that there is power in a family-tree. All I can say is amen, for the internet because there is nothing on there that you cannot find (to a degree) it is an overwhelming place to do research! It makes me more determined to be successful and to succeed in life, though I have always been a hardworking, ambitious lady with plenty actions and realising on my journey so far to simply **'talk less and just do.'** When you hear the name Forbes (straight away), you think of the famous, well-known American Forbes Magazine full of business and wealth by editor-in-chief Steve Forbes.

Whereas my Nigerian side of the family has a surname attached to royalty itself, so both names are extraordinary in my eyes. Identity is important because it teaches us who we are and where we come from, so in writing this book, I wanted first to lay a foundation of who I am and what makes me write and say the things I do. Throughout all my life experiences the 'almighty' has always seen me through and made me think that my turning point in life (maybe) will be in my late thirties.

Whereby I accomplish part of my destiny by finally writing and publishing this first book. Amen

Perhaps I went through what I did growing up so that I would know that love conquers hatred, all day, and every day. Though I do not have any children yet (God willing) when/if I do, I know I will be a caring, loving and probably a strict mum, though, on the other hand, I am very much hoping motherhood will mellow me. Lol! Regardless of the family, you are born into; life is all about creating your own family; only time will tell if I will be so lucky.

Here is one of many voice-messages received during 2016 from my Dad; he always ends the call saying these words, which always makes me smile. I love hearing his voice saying these words to me as they are meaningful and so touching, thank you, Dad, for taking the time to send me voice-messages. This one made me feel more loved by you than I ever did before. x

"Hi Princess, its Dad. I tried calling you but no joy, I hope everything is going ok and work is ok and you're ok. I just want you to know how much I have missed you, miss talking to you and to say I haven't forgotten you. I really, really, really, love you, love you, love you truly and dearly.

I love you with all my body, all my heart, all my mind and soul. I love you from infinity and more than life itself and grateful for all the wonderful things that you have done for me and the way you look after me, you are a proper Daddy's girl and I love you so, so, so, so, so, so,
so, so, so very much princess.

You are the love of my life and I love you dearly and thank our great living-god for blessing me with a wonderful, beautiful, funny, loving, and caring daughter like you. Any father would be proud to call you

his daughter. May God always bless you and I love you lots, and I pray that God continues to shower you with happiness and financial prosperity and the most important thing of all, is good health.

Because without health, money is nothing!
But you know that already.
Hope to talk and see you soon, ok princess.

Love you lots princess and catch up soon, love you".

Words for me have always meant everything because it is much more meaningful and personal, but at the same time a person can say anything and not mean it! Which is why, when it comes to men and relationships it is their <u>actions</u> that need to speak louder than their words! #LoveTheBlackness🖤

Tell Us We Used to Be Barbaric

We Had Actual Queens

Black Is Strugglin'

To Find Your History

Or Trace the Shit You Don't

Know the Truth

About Your Race Cause,

They Erasin' It!!!

Dave '**Black**' Lyrics

Great-Granddad

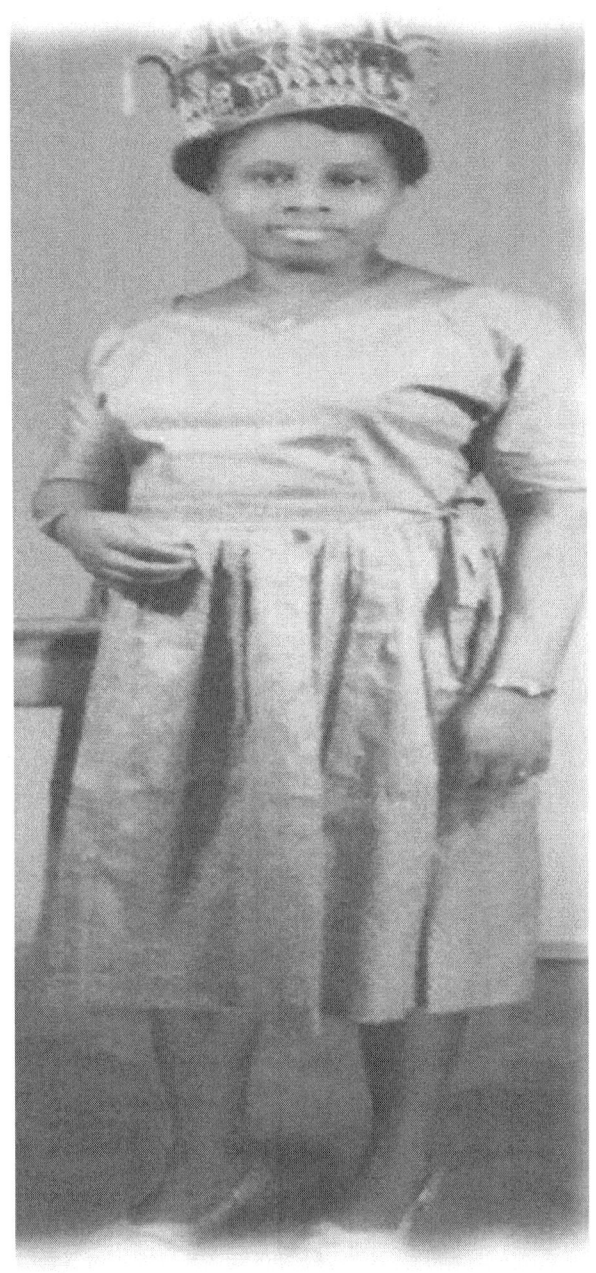

Grandma '**Princess Elizabeth Adebimpe Adepoju** (nee Haastrup).

Great-Granddad on his Throne!

Granddad and Grandma 'Princess Elizabeth Adebimpe Adepoju'

Dad and Me @Grandads 90th in Nigeria '2016

Dad, Me, and my precious Aunt

Cuzie Z and Me

Caron Wheeler (Soul 2 Soul) and Me

Dad, Me and Step-Mum

CHAPTER 4: LADY OF VARIETY

Like most Londoners, I work to sustain myself, to have a roof over my head, invest in me and to live as best as I can! I enjoy writing, listening to music, eating out, volunteering, travelling, watching films and socialising, to name a few. I may be a princess by birth, but it does not bear a resemblance in my everyday life. I have always been a grafter and was not born with a silver spoon in my mouth! I am a self-employed lady with my own Limited Company who has been contracting within the male-dominated world of Construction as a 'Document Controller'. I have no savings or inheritance to fall back on only the money I earn when working along with any paid work gained by any successful auditions and castings.

It all adds up and to submit yourself for work via casting sites like; Spotlight, Starnow, Mandy.com, Casting Now, Stage 32 to name a few, all require monthly subscription fees which all differ. These are all standard sacrifices needed to invest and put yourself out there within the Entertainment Industry. Even if you have an agent, you cannot just rely on them to 'find opportunities' when you are still trying to get that break! So, you must *'keep it moving'* for yourself by applying and putting yourself out there; as you're not the only client on the agents' book.

Back in '2011, I was given the L.I.C (*Lady in Control*) alias name when I was working on 'The Heron' project in Moorgate, London. It was one of the site team members named Mickey Biggs who told me he was the (nephew) of the legendary train robber Ronnie Biggs. I had no reason to believe otherwise! OMG, I could not believe it when he told me.

Working alongside him was guaranteed jokes every day, I even have a pic of him as a souvenir! That is one of the significant advantages of working within this industry because you come across men from all walks of life. In '2006, I started within the construction industry as a Site Secretary a few months after redundancy from a Law Firm in Aldgate, London, after five years of employment. This was my first role being the only female working with all men in the post-room as a 'Fax Operator', so an all-male environment was nothing new to me. Then by '2008, I was also doing the role of a DC (Document Controller), which gave me the option of doing one or the other — sometimes doing a two-in-one by combining both jobs. But only if the agency and client agreed to pay me the same rate from my previous DC role.

Flexibility for me has been a priority because of never knowing when a last-minute audition or job might present itself, which can sometimes come with just a few hours' notice. I am paid by the hour and paid every week, which is what I prefer. Most of all what is there not to love about working with men! There is sometimes eye candy galore, along with banta, casual flirting and all-round laughter which is second to none.

I have no problem putting people (men) mainly in their place whoever they are; I do not care! If I feel like a person has an issue with me, then I will air my grievance and most times being the only female, it comes naturally being able to deal with men. I think most men enjoy it though some could not handle me being able to stand up for myself! But deep in my heart, my main passion is and will always remain within the **Entertainment Industry.** I love the arts! Whether it is Film, Television, Theatre or Reality-TV, I am an avid supporter of most things artistic. I have always loved music and singing along though I do not sing, though some have told me they like my voice, so maybe I am not that bad! Lol.

As a teenager, people complimented me on my slim body and height (5'8) and suggested modelling as a career, so I decided to go ahead and try my hand within the modelling industry. I had my first official photoshoot, aged fifteen back in 1996. What appealed to me most about modelling is that models got to take amazing photos, wear fabulous clothing, their hair and makeup styled by professionals plus travelling to different locations. I admire all the girls, ladies, women, and men who have attained top opportunities and careers as a model. Now there is a 'Curvy' model sector of the industry, which is fabulous and long-awaited! I have always believed.

"If You Don't Try, You Will Never Know"

and had many years of trying though it did not stop me from continuing to have great photoshoots done. My best three photographers to date are from my early twenties by a female at Studio Icon, plus a man called Ben Black. Then my friend from the USA called William Chase @tvpimages who the only person is to have done a photoshoot with me in my thirties back in '2013 which are superb. During my early teens, till now many have been confused by my look, i.e., ethnicity thinking I am either Somalian or Ethiopian.

I can see some of their features in myself and think it is even more unique and beautiful when people assume your ethnicity background, to be **something else!** Modelling was also part of my mum and aunt's life having had some beautiful photos taken during their younger days. I always admired their professional, stunning, sophisticated, and sexy photos. I do not think much has changed within the Modelling Industry regarding females like myself **Ladies of Colour!** They were lacking back in the 9Ts (the 90s) and still now!

There is and has only ever been one prominent Model out of the UK who shines for all 'Black' females, this is the beautiful, forever blessed, never ageing and fabulous supermodel Naomi Campbell who till this day is still going from strength to strength and a great role model. I commented on one of her photos #LoveTheBlackness♥ and was pleased to see that she acknowledged my comment and gave it a 'like', Thank You, Naomi!

When I caught the modelling enthusiasm in my teens, I was applying for all sorts of modelling jobs, from fashion, hand modelling, catalogue to finally glamour work as I knew I 'most definitely' had the assets though it was mainly fake, enhanced models published in all the newspapers and magazines. Over the years I have attended a variety of castings, contacted some well-known agencies, and entered a few top newspaper competitions like Page3, Bust of Britain and FHM (men's magazine) all for the Caucasian female. None of them wanted to show love to anyone who was not pale-skinned or Tanned and if they did, they would add one or two (max) as a way of saying; were not being prejudiced. Joke Business!

Even the Sexiest Women of The Year competitions again were prominently Caucasian females showing that even within Modelling racism has always been present!

Here are two (of my few) rejection letters received from the modelling competitions that I put myself forward for, more than once from two top tabloid Newspapers! A prime example why we (non-Caucasian) females need to be extra thick-skinned when it comes to rejection. I want you to know

"You Are FABULOUS Beyond All Means, But Most of All You Must-Know It Is Not You Whose Lacking Anything.

It Is Merely Because Of The Precious and Blessed Melanin Skin That You Are in Which Has Always Been Frowned Upon, But It Is Their Problem, Not Yours"

#YerISaidIt

These experiences can either make you weaker or stronger. I am glad I have always been a person to keep everything from letters to email as proof of my years of trying within the creative, entertainment industry and these two responses are prime examples of the constant rejection,

The Sun Newspaper

11th April '2000

Nicky Forbes

Dear Nicky
Thank you for sending in your pictures with a view to model for page three.

Your photographs have been carefully considered by our team of experts here, but unfortunately, we do not think you are the right material for this particular paper. I hope you understand that the response to our page three girls is absolutely overwhelming and appreciate that the glamour modelling business is very competitive.

All the best and thank you once again for writing us.

Yours Sincerely

B Goodway
Page 3 Photographer

The Sun

I always thought that this Photographer was a female, how wrong was I! I only done a search of the name on the internet in '2019. He died 4th November '2012, R.I.P. to him.

Daily Star Newspaper

15th August' 2002

Dear Anikka Forbes

Thank you very much for your entry to the Daily Stars Search for a Star Ideal Talent Search. The competition this year was extremely tough with thousands of exceptionally high-quality entries from all over the country. Unfortunately, your look is not quite what we are searching for this time around and we are herewith returning your photos.

Please do not be disheartened by this though - it does not mean you do not have what it takes merely that we are currently after a different style. If you are still interested in pursuing modelling as a career, we recommend you get in touch with either of the two top glamour agencies listed below.

We use both all the time and can vouch for their authenticity.

Y Paul
Tiverton Road
London
NW10

I registered with Model Mayhem in '2006, a casting site for models, aspiring models and professional and amateur photographers. I recommend it as an excellent place to start and network. Again, it was so blatantly evident from applications to castings anything, not Caucasian was irrelevant within the modelling industry! A curvy, black, mixed, caramel-skinned, Lady of Colour like (me) was not 'right', to appear in their magazines, newspapers or even TV. As far as they were concerned, I did not fit their idea of beauty or glamour like the (average) skinny, no shape, standard model. I say this because of how many times I was told.

"You're not what we're looking for"

Those words automatically told me, regardless of what I look like, you are black; therefore, there is no place for you within this industry! Now were in 2016 and for the last few years everyone wants to be looking the same, but it is the replica of the BLACKNESS 'trend' that is the most prominent!

Many want or have gone under the knife to get the standard, natural, Nubian perky big bum, lips, and shape. You only need to look at certain well-known females to see the work they have had done to their face and bodies to look like a black female when we have had these blessed assets and features since day one! Could it also be why they are into black men, who are blessed with delicious full lips and the rest? Most non-black males and females don't want their natural look but the look that is desired by most now 'fullness' in the body. People are going from no lips to **luscious lips** or no bum to **full bum**.'

What is the reason behind all these enhancements to look like someone else other than themselves? I find it amusing while also concerning as someone who was bullied and racially abused during my primary school years and remembers (like yesterday) when our full lips were referred to as 'rubber lips' because they were seen to be too big. But now lip fillers, bum lifts and body sculpting are taking over the world and everywhere you look, there is enhanced (frightening) at times, lips, and bottoms on people like it is the norm. Yet, not once was I given ratings or a chance for my naturalness when applying for castings or modelling jobs, but a fake enhanced Caucasian female gets the opportunity. I cannot win! #LoveTheBlackness♥Love2All

The truth is, no form of enhancements on anyone's face or bodies will ever compare or match that of any natural female regardless of ethnicity. Some say 'fake' is the new 'real' and 'white the new black' I certainly do not agree!

I do know; 'there are too many followers of the fakeness and not enough leaders of the realness.' Here is a prime example of real being mistaken as fake when someone asked me *"are your lips real?"* like FFS (for f*ck sake), what a joke! I know plenty would love to have my full, kissable lips and pay lots to try and accomplish it but do not get it twisted natural features do still exist. The 'blackness' is still lacking in so many things here in the United Kingdom from (Films, Soaps, Commercials, Reality Tv, Presenters, Hosts, Government etc.) and the list goes on. The USA has so much more variety and it is a shame the UK still has a long way to go!

Back in my late teens through to my early twenties, people would say I am the 'Black' version of the well-known British Glamour Model simply because of my big bust which I refer to as **'my girls'.** Why, do I refer to my chest as this because they go everywhere with me, never let me down and their simply **Bustylicious**! Once I did reach out with my (brazen self) to her via Facebook asking if I could do a photo-shoot, knowing full well, it would never happen, but I had nothing to lose so thought why not!

I did not get any response, though a small part of me had hoped that I would be pleasantly surprised and get a reply! Only because she was a new mum with a 'black, mixed-race child' so thought she might be opened to helping an aspiring model like me.

The entertainment industry is highly competitive and has the potential of destroying the lives of those who may be a bit naïve to the ins and outs when it comes to the modelling side of things. I have heard my fair share of stories from others, magazines and on the news about models who were told to lose weight, sexually harassed, scammed, and practically starved themselves to remain thin. To being rejected because of their race or mistreated by some agencies which is no joke! I too have a few modelling scandals and traumatic stories myself from my earlier years, which will only be available to you (the reader) IF I turn my remaining ten-years' worth of raw, real, and honest diary material into two more books.

I recently experienced a scenario back in July '2016. Having been successful with a Canadian International Reality Show Competition, long story short; I had taken some Dominatrix modelling photos back in '2015. At the time of applying for the competition, the pics had slipped my mind; therefore, I had forgotten to mention it in the application and for this error, my place was lastminute.com denied. WTF, I was so upset! I got notified that I had made it as a final contestant, paid for my flights with money I did not really have at the time. Then two weeks before I was due to fly out to Canada, I received two phone calls, then an email informing me that my successful application had been disqualified. Due to one of the photos with me holding a whip in a sexy outfit discovered on the internet, which I had removed in the hope they would change their mind, wishful thinking! The photoshoot and training were done all in one day and I enjoyed having my dominatrix photo-shoot and training experience as a dominant female with my submissive slave!

I had the slave refer to me as Madam Minaj and chose this name because I am a fan and share similarities with the beautiful, magnificent, and talented Nicki Minaj. Nicky is my nickname, and our birth names are similar too, hers is Onika and mine is Anikka. How about that, we have something in common; I salute you. #BlackBarbie

There is no shame nor regret for trying it out because in modelling or anything in life, sometimes you do have to push the boundaries. Even the First Lady of the United States is a former model, and she may have done some photo-shoots that could have raised a few eyebrows, but none the less she still rose into a compelling position in America. People who judge a model over photos that they find to be 'too revealing' or a female in general who likes to take sexy or daring pics are the overly judgmental types! They need to get a grip on reality, move with the times and the world we live in today but most of all we all have a body, some enjoy taking photos and some do not, simple! It is all about embracing self-love for ourselves. We are not in the Victorian age where all women had no control over themselves, image, or mind. For those covered head to toe to be respected or out of respect (something required) by some faiths which I understand! Does not mean I agree with the double-standards that some men have over females!

In modelling, you must be open and sometimes daring to test or push yourself and break out of your comfort zone. So, this is precisely what I did when I decided to do a dominatrix photo-shoot with the beautiful, voluptuous Madam C, the black goddess aka 'queen in control' of Dominatrix and could not have asked for a better teacher! You may be asking yourself,

> *"Anikka, you're of an African Royal Bloodline and technically an actual princess, why would you do such a thing?"*

Well, the simple answer to that is my modelling has been a part of my life since my teens and only found out about my royal bloodline three-years ago! Do I think had I known what I know now from a young age it would have been different? Honestly, I do not know, maybe or maybe not!

A **'Lady of Variety'** is how I have summed myself up since '2017. An open-minded person who has had a great variety of jobs over the years ranging from; Retail, Sales, Capsule Host (London Eye), Personal Assistant, Carer, Appropriate Adult, Hostess, Family Contact Supervisor to name a few. Why have I gone between so many different job sectors over the years? The answer is they are all jobs that I either wanted to try and the rest came my way so gave them ago! I have learnt a lot from them, met great people over the years too while continuing to pursue a career within entertainment. When I am in front of a camera, on-stage performing in a play or recording a vlog I just come alive.

I think this love of the spotlight is innate in me, so perhaps it comes from my ancestors who were royalty and were the center of attention in their region. They were honored and upheld in high esteem by the locals. Now that I have reconciled with my Dad and finally experienced my first visit to Nigeria, which I thought would (never) happen. Then to find out my family heritage was an extraordinary one and wish I could go back in time to when my Grandma was a young princess wearing her crown. Magical! Women are often expected to conform to societal rules and regulations in their everyday life, my experiences and what I have seen growing up has molded me.

I would say the core reason for my stern persona (at times) mainly towards men – is because of living through mums' on and off toxic relationship for years. Instead, I would rather stick with my firm, hard to read personality than be timid! I am thankful not to have been influenced by such thinking. As a female of African descent, I am fully aware of the obstacles we face and must overcome in a male-controlled and racist world.

The oppression the African woman has had to endure the past two millenniums has come at a hefty price. So much so that it will take a lot of resources to help put her back in her rightful place with honour and respect. Perhaps there has never been a more oppressive system in place for African women than the slavery system of the United States, which black Americans had to endure for 246 years.

When African women were being captured along the coast and within the interior of Africa during the **Transatlantic Slave Trade**, she had no idea what awaited her and her descendants. Most times she was raped before ever entering the slave ships and her breasts were branded with hot irons, as you would cattle signifying ownership. She was no longer a proud, beautiful woman but dehumanised as cattle or a sexual tool. Plantation life for her was not much more manageable once she arrived in the west.

She endured being forced to nurse and for the most part, be a surrogate mother to the children of her master and his wife as well as bear his children too! Her working days were as long as eighteen hours picking cotton under the hot sun or cleaning and cooking. As if that was not enough, she had to endure the sexual exploits of her slave master against her will. Even girls as young as nine years old and younger were victims of rape. I know the obstacles I have endured so far in my life, even more so as a **'Lady of Colour'**.

My pursuit of a modelling career crossed into acting. I also had a few one-to-one acting lessons with actress Karen Henthorn back in '2005, she played the character Teresa Bryant in Coronation Street back in 2007/8. I have also had some television, theatre, and feature film work over the years. I admire all actresses and actors as learning scripts is incredibly challenging (for me), but once done and you transform into a character it is an amazing and proud feeling. A fabulous throwback moment that I am in awe of till this day is back in my early twenties when I had someone a French fine young man named Jibril who I met while assisting as the (artist coordinator) at my friend Tasha's music company called Urban Kingdom back in 2002/3.

He had joined as one of the Artist and we got on well and had great chemistry. I did not believe him at first when he told me that he had written a song called 'Nicky' for me until he played it and I was gobsmacked and overwhelmed, like WOW. Really for me! How many people can say someone took the time to think and write a song then record it and make it officially for you. HEY, I can. The wickedest thing is he was, and I am sure still is a fine man!

As much as I was attracted to him and there was chemistry between us, I did not allow myself to test the waters. I kept it professional and did not **mix business with pleasure**, a rare man he is indeed! I do not think another man can top this, as writing and recording a song for a female is a one-off, unique gift. Thank you again, Jibril, for this song you will always have that unique place in my heart. ♀

Tuesday 10th November '2015: Below, a post that I put on my Instagram of the word 'Reality' and how I sum it up.

R: Real
E: Easy-going
A: Ambitious
L: Lovely
I: Individual
T: Too Honest 4 My Own Good
Y: Yer I Said It

Then the (primary) reality experience that I longed for, for the longest time, having applied and auditioned over 12 times out of the eighteen years that it had aired on tv, with my final solo attempt back in '2016, when I submitted my best audition to date. I went that extra mile by having it filmed and edited professionally, thanks to an old-housemate Ignazio and his wife. This video was a creative montage which I put a lot of thought into for it to be right, I even decided to add my 'random' little rap which just popped into my head back in '2011.

It is called **Ms. U.S.B** (ultra, sexy, babe) another alias name, was added at the end of the montage! I was given the Ms. U.S.B name, back in '2006 when I started my first construction job as a Site Secretary with 'Bowmer and Kirkland by the Site Manager. He named me this because I always used my USB (Universal Serial Bus) stick, which was on my bunch of keys. A big thank you (not that he had much choice) Lol - to Lorenzo, another one of my ex-housemates for featuring in my 'just-for-fun' music video, so, have you guessed what reality tv show I am talking about, yep it is Big Brother UK. Lorenzo and I also auditioned as a duo back in '2017.

This was officially my last attempt and still never made it into the house.

Interestingly, last year they had a black mother and daughter in the house and back in '2008 I auditioned with my mum; this (audition) is viewable on one of my two YouTube Channels called **The ChatBack Show.** Plus, they also had a 'royal heir' in the house too, again having also included my own African Royal Bloodline in my '2016 video audition. No matter my honesty, realness or being told by the production team and producers how great and feisty they thought I was; they still never selected me. At least I kept trying though unsuccessful! Maybe Big Brother could not handle the R.E.A.L.I.T.Y me!!! Or perhaps it was my past debts (just being honest). If they did any credit checks on me, it might have flagged up, so that might have been a **no go** for them which I understand! #IAmWorthy

Though in all honesty, when I think about it, I have already been living the Big Brother experience, real-life version a million-per cent authentic and unedited since moving to west London in '2011. Would you believe I have house-shared and lived with over forty housemates from all parts of the world since '2013? I have moved and lived at a total of **27** different postcodes around South-East and West London over the last thirty-six-years of my life.

Twelve times in South-East and fifteen times in West London. At one point in June '2013, I had to move from where I was living in Chiswick a week before moving in with my Bessie-mate Christian for a while.

I looked on Gumtree and saw a room-share paying £200 a month, so I contacted the person and explained I only needed the room for a weekend he (landlord) agreed that it was okay for me to stay and pay

£50 and to cut another long story short I had to share his double bed with him!

WHAT, Lol, I can hear you say! Yes, I know it is not the norm and my previous room-share experiences had two separate beds (first time for everything). He was a gentleman in his sixties, I was made to feel at home and for that week, I mainly had the room to myself. He slept under his duvet and I slept on top of the duvet under my own covers safe and sound. There was another female tenant, renting his spare room though I only saw her once within the week of me living there. Trust me had I felt any sort of uncomfortableness when I viewed the flat, I would never have moved in, but all was good, thank god! So, in all honesty, Big Brother was not ready for me Anikka Forbes! I have lived it but without the cameras. #IAmReality

My last Theatre acting experience was back in 2012, written and directed by Lorna Blackman. The name of the production was called **Good Black Men and Good Black Women.** It was a variety of sketches involved in the overall play. I loved the sketch 'cold face' that she wrote for me, the detail in the way she perceived me as to why she gave it that name. I agree the title summed me up exactly right as I am sure many would agree that my face can come across as cold or hard to read! A southern-American accent is what came out of my mouth when I first performed the lines and that is what I used when performing the sketch live in front of an audience, which took me out of my comfort zone! I worked alongside a great cast and still in contact with a few from there. There was two who stood out from them all one being Daniel and the other who is, undoubtedly a 'man of variety' whose creative, handsome, talented, and super funny. Check him out Samuel you will not be disappointed! @ogasamuel

I also had the opportunity to appear in a music video which my agent (at the time) Jack Bypass put me forward for and it was an enjoyable experience back in '2014. Though at first, I did not recognize the artists' name until I had done my research on the internet. Then I listened to one of his well-known songs Let Her Go, which sold over a million copies back in December 2013, it was a song I liked hearing on the radio but did not know he sang it!

The much loved and talented artist was **'Passenger'** aka Michael David Rosenberg. What a charming and cool man he is and so down to earth! He introduced himself, socialized with us all and made everyone on his video-shoot, feel at ease. The filming outside in the big, open field/forest was not glamorous, but the weather was superb. Everyone involved was proud to have had the experience, even though I nearly got eaten alive in the bushes, Lmfao! It was well worth it even more so once the final edit was done, I got to see it for the first time when it was aired on the music channels and YouTube called **Passenger Scare Away the Dark**. I am a believer that people should do or at least try to do whatever they enjoy!

I love the entertainment industry and will always put myself forward for any opportunities by continuing to put myself out there, for anyone of interest to see. Both YouTube Channels Anikka Forbes and The ChatBack Show (where anything goes) are full of variety, as you will see if you decide to check either one of them out! Being an open individual who is always trying something new is just how I do, which is not for everyone! Though I have tried sticking to one, then found myself branch off in another direction; it is all entertainment and creativity.

My twenty-years plus of 'trying' is clearly shown if you 'google' my name it is not that much, but it is something. Proof that I have been putting myself out there on the big wide web for a while! Entertainment is variety, which is me and many are unaware of this side of my life, well, until now!

I can freely express every aspect of who I am as an independent, hard-working, courageous shy (at times) vulnerable person, believe it or not!

Pursuing what makes you happy is necessary as long, as it does no harm. The same way you do not want to do anything which might leave you feeling ashamed later in life apart from that, **be yourself** and **stay true to you**! It has never been about just doing for myself but also giving back to the community like those that are homeless, as they are the vulnerable ones who most of the time do not have a safe place to sleep at night.

I prefer to give a homeless person food direct instead of money, which I have done on many occasions on my way to or from work by popping into a supermarket, buying a meal deal, and giving it to the person.

Then in '2013 during the Christmas period I volunteered at Crisis instead of being at home I went to give a helping hand to this great charity, where I got to work, meet new people but most of all sit, talk and listen to those who were living on the streets. This experience then made me think of creating another Channel on YT dedicated to the homeless called 'Homeless We Are Worthy' giving them a voice to share their stories, express what help, and ideas they have for more to be done to help them. So many times, people walk past a person on the street as if they are not there and the view of some homeless people that I have spoken too, is that it makes them feel invisible!

Anyway, when I was living in Fulham, I would go driving around in the middle of the night to see if I could find any homeless people who did not mind sharing their personal experiences and as a thank you; I paid them £10 for their time. I managed to speak to two or three people one was a female and as she was sharing her story, I was near to tears as it just hit my heart to know that homelessness can affect anyone, and I thank god that my near experience of nearly being on the street too did not get that far. I give thanks every day I wake to have a roof over my head. Do I sometimes get fed-up, disheartened, and lost with myself? YES, I do! Because I am only human. And though having variety is excellent, it is not when you feel like doors still are not opening after years of trying! That is when the devil is ready to pounce with the self-doubt of

"What am I doing with my life"

And feeling lost! It is certainly NOT how I expected to be feeling in my late thirties, but it is true! I can only hope that by the time this book is finally published my view on my direction in life will be more evident, by god's grace. Amen

Being self-employed has its disadvantage because if I do not work, I do not make money, nor do I get holiday or sick pay. I prefer the flexibility and I know I can be very headstrong within the construction industry and take no prisoners. I have been told a few times over the years about work colleagues whining about my emails being too 'outspoken 'and my response has always been

"As long as I am not disrespectful, swearing or impolite"

Then I will always express myself! On occasions, I have left and moved on to another project when I have felt like my hard work and my many hours of overtime was not appreciated and never looked back! Though there is one or two, I wish I had not been so hasty or stubborn and should have remained working on the project. The construction industry is full of variety and no two tradespeople are the same. Sometimes we do things either in the spare of the moment, to try a different avenue or simply because it is something you have always wanted to try! Either way, there is nothing wrong with that in my opinion. Too many people leave this world unfulfilled and unhappy because they regret not doing more or trying new things. That is so not going to be me. I hope!

I still have plenty I want to do, other personal projects I want to pursue, travel more, and write more but most of all above everything else I hope one day to have a child or children, by Gods' Grace. Until then, I will continue to take each day as it comes, simply (doing me) plus sharing another hobby of mine which I have always loved Photography.

#TheLICPhotography is what I was using previous but have now changed it to #AnikkaForbesPhotography after all my name is my **Brand** which I have been using from day one alongside Nicky Forbes at times. A variety of past, present and new photos taken by me and my creative eye! For anyone who also loves snapping and wants to share their photos, I would recommend as I am a big fan of 'Guru Shots'.

It is an excellent site to showcase all your photography passion. I am also enjoying using the 'Southeast Asia Live Streaming App' called **BIGO** since November '2018 having been introduced to it by TMA Talent Management. You can broadcast live to the world your daily activities with mine mainly chatting with the viewers/fans playing music and working out. You can also watch other people's broadcast, receive, or give virtual gifts while building a fan base. My Anikka Forbes fan base currently stands at 23.1k. But it is now suspended, due to the lack of love for 'People of Colour' I had even dedicated a fan page direct on my website as a thank you to all the fans for their love, support, and gifts.

If you were to ask me what one great opportunity, I would like to come from writing my memoir in the hope that many all over the world will be a #ImAFan (I'm Anikka Forbes Fan) including any of these Talk Show hosts like; Wendy Williams, Jonathan Ross, or Ellen DeGeneres.

Oprah, though she is no longer doing her talk show but will always be the queen of talk shows. I love her series Greenleaf and Queen Sugar too! I am a big fan of you all and enjoy watching your talk show. But most of all I am ready for an **invite** to appear on any of your shows. Thank you in advance! #JustSaying 🙇‍♀️

Like most, I have had many times of feeling disappointed for not being selected for specific auditions. But it would not take long for me to brush it off with the best reverse psychology thought of

"It is their loss, not mine"

Then my confidence would rise back up, harder, and even more thick-skinned ready to tackle the next opportunity. Though most of my life has been full of rejection from my childhood, I have kept going! If I gave up every time, I received a rejection for <u>something I wanted</u> I would not have written this book! I believe enough in my truth along with my (honesty, realness, and words) when it comes to writing.

So, if nothing else comes of my life for me to be a million-per cent proud of, then officially completing this book and self-publishing it is a great achievement but to have it as a top-seller plus published by a bookstore would be the (icing on the cake) and ultimate accomplishment!

NO ONE can ever say that I Anikka Forbes aka Nicky was.

"All Talk and no Action"

Or that I gave up on anything without trying my utmost best! #YerISaidIt

YOU BECOME WHAT YOU

BELIEVE NOT WHAT YOU

WISH OR WANT BUT

WHAT YOU TRULY BELIEVE

Oprah

First Photoshoot aged 15 back in 1996.

Think this was during my late teens

Photographer: Osman Deen | *Year:* 2002-2003

Photographer: Ben Black | **Year:** 2002-2004

The Journey of a Hidden Princess | #TJOAHP

Photographer: *Female* | ***Year:*** *2004-2006*

Photographer: *Female* | ***Year:*** *2004-2006*

Photographer: Osman Deen | *Year:* 2002-2003

Photographer: Ben Black | *Year:* 2002-2004

Feature: The Pride Magazine | **Year:** 2003

Photographer: Female | **Year:** 2004-2006

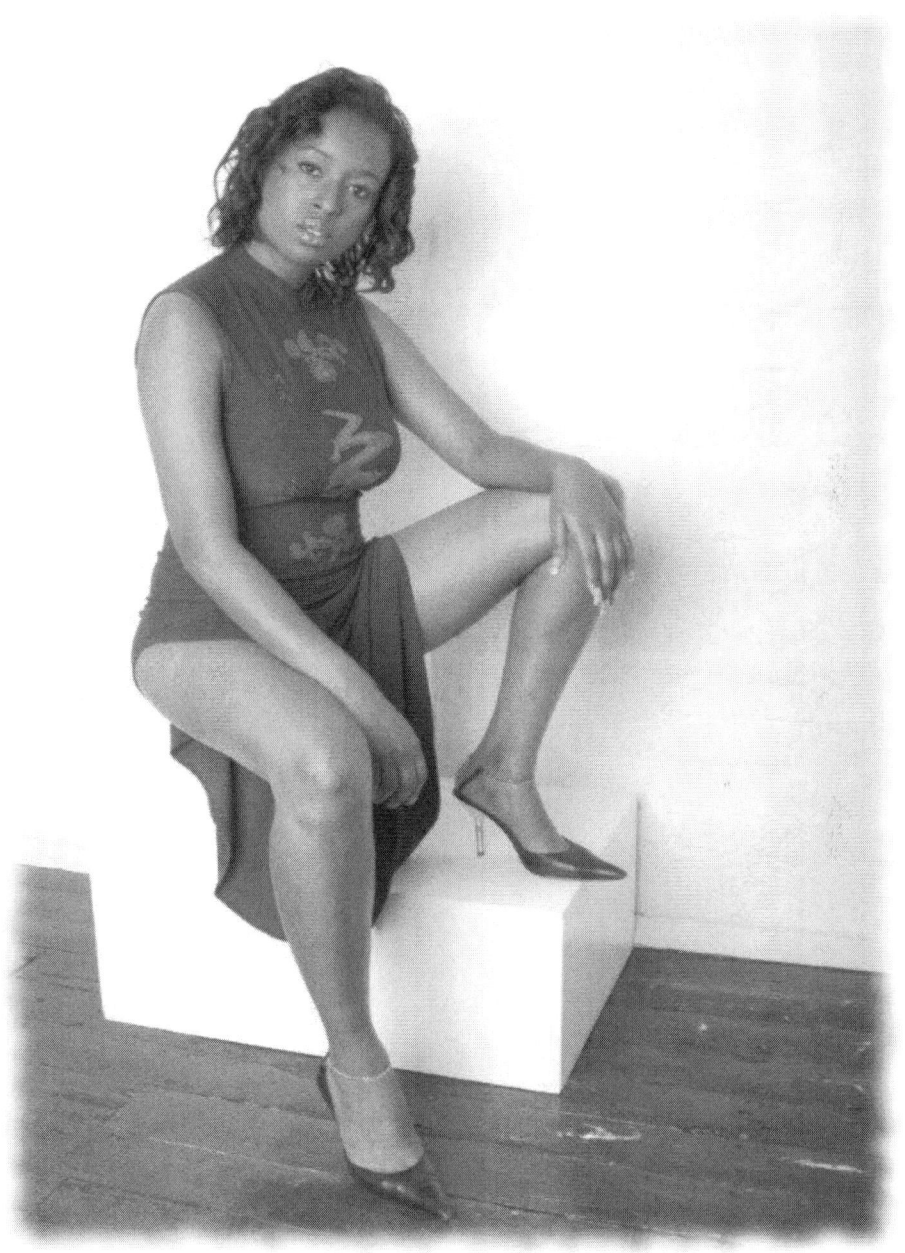

Photographer: *Female* | **Year:** *2004-2006*

11th April 2000

Nicky Forbes
Bellingham Road
Catford
London
SE6 1EQ

Dear Nicky

Thank you for sending in your pictures with a view to modelling for Page 3.

Your photographs have been carefully considered by our team of experts here, but unfortunately we do not think you are the right material for this particular paper.

I hope you understand that the response to our Page 3 girls is absolutely overwhelming and appreciate that the glamour modelling business is very competitive.

All the very best and thank you once again for writing to us.

Yours sincerely,

Page 3 Photographer
The Sun

Encl.

Original Letter '2002

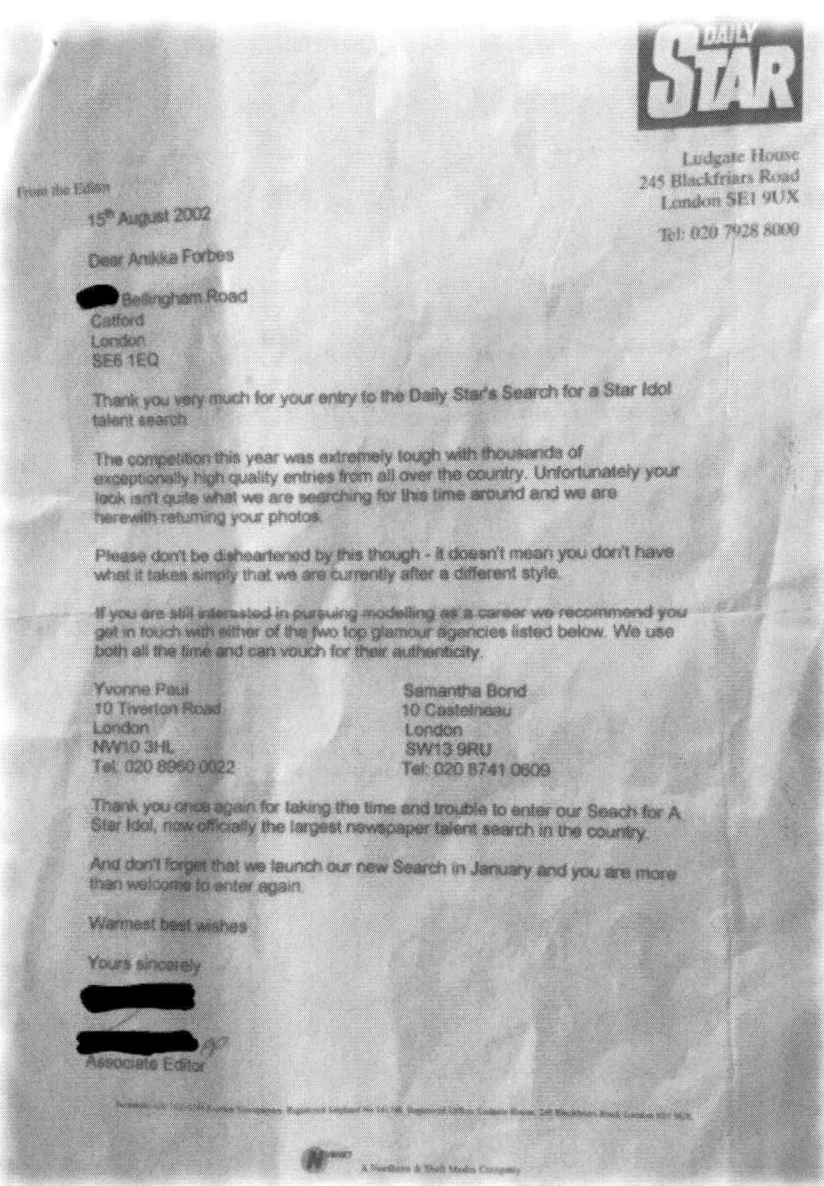

Original Letter '2002

On 29th Feb '12 I performed for the 1st time in
'Good Black Men & Good Black Women'
at the Westminster College.

We had Mr Glen Yearwood of BET UK, in the audience.
I was one of the few Cast Members he gave a
Personal Review. Here is what he said;

The voluptuous woman who
'Could talk with her eyes'
Was for me the hidden gem of the
Female cast. Might be a male thing but
I would venture to say she was a natural.

Mr. Yearwood

Photographer: Ben Black | **Background Change:** John Foscolos

Photographer: Chase @tvpimages | **Year:** 2013

Photographer: *Chase @tvpimages* | **Year:** *2013*

Photographer: *Chase @tvpimages* | **Year:** *2013*

Photographer: Chase @tvpimages | **Year:** 2013

Photographer: Chase @tvpimages | **Year:** *2013*

Photographer: *Chase @tvpimages* | **Year:** *2013*

Photographer: Chase @tvpimages | **Year:** 2013

Anikka Forbes Photography

Theatre Performance: *IDS (Identity Drama School)* | **Year:** *2011*

Anikka Forbes Photography

Theatre Production: *Good Black Men & Good Black Women '2012*

Anikka Forbes Photography

Headshots Photographer: | Year: 2013/14

Cast Member Interview: *Ben TV*

On-Set: *Michael David Rosenberg aka Passenger*

New Acting Headshots '2019

New Acting Headshots '2019

CHAPTER 5: NIECE, CRETE, ATTACK

Friday 1st May' 2015

HOLIDAY!!!! 7.20 am, awake and decide to re-pack my suitcase, this time with only 14 items (plus two more items) as you do. Lol!!! Wash my few dishes and make sure the place is tidy for when I return home on Saturday 9th, I jump in the shower, get sorted and out the door just after 10 am. Can you believe it, there is me thinking I am running on good Time'age when the truth is, I end up returning home twice having walked 5mins down the road and realised I had forgotten my glasses?

Then the second time, I forgot the padlock for my suitcase. 😊 KMT! So, I finally get to East Acton station at 10.30 am and while waiting for the tube to arrive I start checking my emails and was pleasantly surprised'ish (meaning I was but I was not) when I saw an email from the Agency, I got the contract with which reads.

Anikka
P (company) have informed me today that they do not want you to return. Please give me a call when you are available, and we will look for alternative roles for you.

Regards
J

Surprised.com, no, I was not! If anything, I find it a joke. Because no one was man enough to tell me directly to my face yesterday when I was at work instead, they wait until I am going on holiday to inform the agency so that they can notify me!!! How fucking cowardly are these men on this project, complete and utter jokers? I was disappointed by the PM (project manager) as we got on well, or so I thought! He talked to me about his mum, kids and was generally a sweet man but obviously, a few of the guys found me hard to handle. LMFAO!!! Anyway, I decided to send my response straight back to the PM at work.

Hi ___, I have just been informed about my services no longer being required which is fine. As I do not expect weak and dishonest men to handle a strong, outspoken lady like myself who speaks the truth and does my job well!!! I have been with ___ on two-projects for 7mths and should have been informed by someone yesterday (as my last working day in the office), so I could have cleared out my few personal belongings in my locker and returned a few items. Therefore, as I was not given appropriate notice, so I could clear my stuff I will return to give back the locker keys (once I have removed my few bits) and hand-back the laptop which is also in the locker. Last but not least, get my Timesheets signed when I get back from holiday. Thanks

So, end of a contract, the only female (standard) on the project who was no push-over, too honest, truthful, and outspoken! For me, there is no better way to forget about that project than to go on holiday for a refreshing break then return home for my new chapter as a #LadyofLeisure while looking for a new contracted job and waiting to see what's around the corner awaiting me! I want (putting it out there to the universe) fabulous opportunities to present themselves as of July/Aug onwards. I pray to God it is to do with either acting or reality tv, though I well and know it certainly is not going to be Big Brother.

I arrive at Victoria Coach Station just after 11 am while 'J' (Jeyda) my beautiful niece, is on her way to meet me at about 11:40 am. It was so great to see the little darling, though I was not impressed with her orange-face looking like some Umpa-Lumpa. Lol!!! I tell her about the email I just received from the agency along with my reply and we both start laughing. We get the coach to Gatwick (South) Terminal just after 1 pm when I nearly have a mini panic attack. Why? Because I still had not checked us in and we were boarding soon, nor had I bothered to print off the boarding passes. WTF, scatty-brain or what!!! Amen for the Easyjet App, which I had previously used but had forgotten my password (Long). So, I had to reactivate it, check us in which then automatically activated our boarding passes. #CreteHereWeCome

My niece has her bag held to the side and asks the security person

"why is my bag getting searched"

She sounds so innocent and cute; then she finds out why – because she had put her perfume in her hand luggage, instead of her suitcase. So, had to leave it behind among the many items that get confiscated by security, that are not permitted. I am sure every day must feel like Christmas for them! 😁 By the time we arrived safe and sound at the stunning hotel, it was after midnight. The next day I and J wake up, to start getting sorted then she tells me she had forgotten her toothbrush! Standard hygiene was always an issue for my niece, so not surprised. I was far from impressed when I ask her.

ME: *"So, what did you use"?*

and she tells me

NIECE: *"I used a 'wipe' to clean my teeth"!*

Firstly, I thought there are not any wipes only the Andrex toilet wipes and secondly what about her morning breath (though I wanted to say something) I did not because I knew it would only make her vex! I did not pay for her to come on her first holiday abroad for any foolishness, other than good times. So, I tell her to 'put some toothpaste on her finger' and use the mouthwash then buy a toothbrush when we are out, sorted! Once she had finished, we head out to have breakfast and see the couple (from next door) who we met on our arrival to the hotel and had a few drinks and a laugh. Last night when we were socialising with them, someone popped their head out their door to ask us to **"keep the noise down"**, (bloody cheek) were on holiday, after all!

I ate breakfast, my belly was full then sat chilling awhile looking out at the stunning ocean when on the way back to our room we stop in the shop within the hotel so 'J' could buy a toothbrush. We decided to get changed into our swimwear (excited.com) to be wearing my custom-made swimsuit; it looked great on! 😉 Then I went outside our door to lay in the fabulous sun on the sun lounger. #LoveIt

Just after 3 pm, we go for lunch and I notice she is putting loads of food on her plate but not eating it as we're sitting down at the table, so when I ask her why she is wasting so much food, her response is she does not like it!!! Does my niece have an eating disorder along with her other issues?

Only God knows but most def 'got my eye on her' whether she likes it or not. Then she starts complaining about the staff, how their getting stressed and if it were her, she would not be if she worked there. Then she tried comparing the five* hotel we were staying at to Costa Coffee where she worked which is when I had to shut-her-down by letting her know that she cannot compare both! I saw that she had recently updated her status on WhatsApp saying.

"Don't know why I bother,
It ain't gonna work so might as well give up"

I did not bother asking her about it as I assume it is about a boy. Here she is on an all paid for All-Inclusive Holiday and she is wasting her time writing wasteful and unhappy messages rather than enjoying her time away. It is not a good look, nor am I feeling her negative, ungrateful vibes. Later that evening we end up meeting with our old neighbours who had moved rooms in the bar in the hotel to have a few drinks (a Pina colada and a few shots). We are all talking when the Entertainer who we met earlier in the day comes over to speak and he ends up joining us for a while. He is a hilarious guy, that loves himself (which is all good) as he is a handsome, charming person who I could tell from his body language and chat, had taken a shine to me!

But I made out like I was non-the-wiser. He and J were talking before they decided to go and have a smoke. I could hear him telling her that she is sweet and beautiful as a little sister. As soon as J came back inside, she comes straight over to whisper in my ear that she thinks he likes me; unaware that I had overheard their conversation. After 11 pm, we end up moving outside (so the smokers) could smoke while we continue talking. J, is back on the phone to her one friend, chatting the same dry chat until she decides to go into the disco room and make friends with the DJ! At about 12.30 am, I go and join her, there was only J and the DJ. inside.

Mr DJ played a few tunes, so I took it upon myself to make the most of the empty space, leaving them to continue talking and getting to know each other. By 01:00 am the music was turned off, but none of us was ready for bed yet. So, the three of us plus the couple (as you can see) I am terrible with names and cannot remember theirs. Lol! We decide to go down to the bar on the beach and have a few Tequilas. It is about 4 am when the couple and I are more than ready to head back to our rooms, but 'J' was not ready to leave, so I told her I was ok with her staying a little longer only if 'Mr. DJ.' would bring her back safe and sound, which he (agreed) he would do! 'J' was not mashed (drunk) just cheerful plus a little merry and having a good time.

Trust me, had I not thought she was sober enough or had given me any signs that she was vulnerable I would have taken her straight home with me when I was leaving. The girlfriend of the 'couple' was the only super mashed one out of the four of us; she was so lean-up that when she went to jump on her boyfriend's back, she forgot to hold on tight so ended up falling backwards and smashed her head on the concrete floor. OMFGG!

I am shitting myself thinking she is badly hurt (but she reassures us) that she is ok which is when I tell her boyfriend not to let her fall asleep straight away, as that's the worst thing a person can do when they have suffered a hard hit to the head. We passed my room first, so I say my goodbyes and they head off down to theirs a few mins walk from me and I get in, undress and it is straight into bed. An hour or so later, she returns, so I open the door for her and climb back in bed to go to sleep! Then two-twos I heard the door open and close along with some whispering, so I turn around and there is my niece with the DJ guy standing face to face in the dark by the door. This convo is a mixture of what I remembered and what I recorded on my phone after she attacked me!

ME: *"Do you think I can't hear you, what are you doing"?*

NIECE: *"Nothing, I have just come to get something."*

ME: *"To get what"?*

NIECE: *"To get something."*

ME: *"Look, just go back and sit outside or come in and go to bed."*

NIECE: *"Oh just go back to sleep Aunty Nicky"*

ME: *"What do you mean go back to sleep when the two of you have just come in the room! What are you doing, please"?*

NIECE: *"I have come to get something!"*

ME: *"To get what"?*

NIECE: *"Something".*

ME: *"Either go back outside and sit down or come to bed. Don't let me get up"!*

NIECE: *"And what!!!? Get up then."*

So, I do and walk over to them by the door. I tell him to leave and he will see her tomorrow and for her to go to bed. But she did not want to listen to me; instead, she was trying to get Renk (rude and out of order). As I am opening the door to see Mr DJ out, there she is trying to leave with him, so I put my hand out to hold her back and then she pushes me, so I move her away from the door and before I know it, she is hitting out at me! I manage to push her back away from the door again straight onto the bed, trying to hold her so that she can calm down. Then she starts kicking me. WTF! What is going on with this child please (I was thinking) she is like a 'mad' gyal (girl) all because I did not allow her to keep the boy in the room or should I say,

"I mashed up any antics that she was looking to go on wid"

In my presence? Nah mate was not happening!!! I was glad that I did not lose it as the last time I had a physical fight; it was with my older brother (her Dad) in the mid-90s during my early teens. We were fighting so bad that I pushed him hard (not realising) where he was standing, he fell back then went flying, crashing through the glass window, onto the front lawn. #thankgod

Whenever we use to fight it was far from pretty and had I lost it with her trust me she would have been seriously hurt, lost at sea or dead!!! Because outside our room was the pool then 3 meters away was the edge leading to the deep blue sea so was not about to be responsible for her half off-key self with some alcohol in her system to fall into either of those two places. I had to try my hardest to keep her inside though she was fighting and cussing as I have never seen before! Then she manages to push me off her and runs straight out the door. I jump up, run after her then give a big push hoping to slow her down or make her fall over, so she would not run off. It works, she falls then ends up perching on the edge of the next-door neighbour's wall which is when her mouth started unleashing all her truth and real thoughts about me her 'aunty', with the added help of any additional alcohol that she'd drunk once I would left.

NIECE: *(shouting)* *"I did not even wanna come on this holiday, I don't know why I came"!*

ME: *"You joker, so what did you come for I did not beg you to come"!!!*

NIECE: *"I came because I felt sorry for you, you ain't got no 1, no family, no friends, no one likes you cause you're too rude! Look at you; you are in west London all by yourself. Look you even said, "let see if we can make some friends on holiday and I am you're get up and go".*

ME: *"'J' you're sick! How you are feeling sorry for me when I removed myself away from the family drama in South-East London to West London to start anew. As for the "let's see if we meet new people" that is what you do on holiday. And yes, I did say "you're my get up and go" because you ain't got no responsibilities and ur 17 so who would not want to be their aunts' occasional travel buddy. Seriously you're not well"!!*

NIECE: *"Look even Christian called your mum to say you would not move out of his home, not even he wanted you there! You are there with some old man, look at you. You are nasty!!! Even Nanny does not like you! You have nothing"! "They even fired you from your job cause you're too rude"!!!*

ME: *"So they don't want me back because I am a realist who says how it is; not like you and your fake arse self!!! I thought you were like me, but you ain't as I don't go around attacking people, nor am I fake you* *have the cheek to say you feel sorry for me, don't make me laugh! Look at you, a 17yr old whose been kicked out of your home having been removed by police for putting your hands on your mum. You are then locked up overnight (twice)! Not even your own Nan (my mum) cared about you, which is why she did not go to the police station when you called her! No one came but your one friend's mum, who in the end also ended up <u>kicking you out</u> too.*

Why because you are off-key, you try to enter our room with that boy and do what, please!!! You think you can come on holiday (your 1st official holiday) which I do not see anyone else asking or paying for you to go on! But you think you can go away with me ya aunty and try to carry on 'Loose'? Nar sorry mate, ain't happening".

NIECE: *"I don't even like you; look at you. You ain't no aunty of mine, look at your breast just hanging out down to the floor".*

ME: *"Don't hate, cause you ain't got none. You got the cheek to say look at me! Look at you with ya half saggy skin that you're always complaining about and ya nasty self you come on holiday, forget ya toothbrush and instead of using the toothpaste and ya finger you decide to use toilet wipes instead. Your too nasty J, you got a cheek"!!!*

NIECE: *"Look at you and ya saggy breast ya black cunt, I don't even like black people"!!!*

(WTF. She had gone to a whole new disgraceful level.
What was I hearing, please?)

ME: *(Laughing) "Don't make me laugh!!! What do you mean you do not like black people, hello ya Dad's black, your half black, you idiot"!*

NIECE: *"I don't care, I ain't black look, look at my skin Colour, what Colour is it"?*

ME: *"You tell me"!*

NIECE: *"No, you look and tell me! And why did you tell that guy to come and meet us for a drink."*

ME: *"What do you mean, I told him when he is not working, he should join us for a drink. Why not. I did not ask him to come to our room, so what the fuck you talking about"!!!*

By this time, the neighbour whose room she was outside came out for about 5mins with his phone in his hand; I swear he was filming us, but I did not pay him much mind. I would not blame him if he did as I wish I had too! She finally gets up, heads back inside and I follow. Her mouth is still running and then before I know it, she is walking over to her side of the bed, yanks the lovely lamp out of the wall and throws it in my direction. It smashes on the floor; glass is everywhere. At this point, I pick up the phone to call reception to tell them what is happening and the damages that she is causing in our room as there was no way I was going to be paying for anything!

A few minutes go by and someone comes down. One of the hotel workers (male) comes in while I am on the phone to her Mum explaining what her child had done. I tried calling her Dad 1st, but his phone was off and so had to call her mum instead. The 'hotel worker' sees all the mess on the floor! I inform him what has happened, and he can see all the glass and the torn curtain. I start explaining to him that she had caused all the damage to the room which I would not be paying for and wanted him to know! While I was talking to him, she is on the phone crying and sobbing to her mum like Ms Innocent. Then switches to an angry and aggressive tone which she carries on throughout her convo with her mum, it was alarming in a proper possessed type of way, as she is changing between 2-3 personalities.

NIECE: *"I need to book a flight".*

(I get up to go toilet and see what she has done to me! Scratched up my neck, face, and arm)

NIECE: (on the phone to her mum) *"I need to go home. I just came to put my coat on cause I was freezing I just wanted to put a coat on, all I wanted to do was get a coat and she is calling me loose. I did not do anything! I just need to come back to London. All I wanted to do is put my coat on. All I did was come in to get my jacket, so I was not cold outside".*

HOTEL WORKER: *"You two were fighting"?*

ME: *"She was trying to fight with me."*

NIECE: (in the background) *"Mum she told me I was being loose because I brought my friend in the room".*

ME: *"Err hello, do you see any marks on her (I say to the Hotel Worker) it is me only"?*

NIECE: *"Yes, I got marks on my knees, on my legs, on my arms."*

ME*:* *"She came in here with the D.J. guy and I told her to tell him to go and come to bed, but she was not having it".*

NIECE: (Getting aggressive) *"She tried to… please, mum, can you book me a flight home now."*

ME: *"She is mashed up the curtain, the lamp."*

NIECE: (more aggressive*) "Book me a flight home mum, mum I need to come home. No, Mum, I need to come home now".*

ME: *(to hotel worker) "Be-careful before she tries fighting you too."*

NIECE: (Crying again) *"Mum, I need to come home Mum, you need to book me a flight home… you need to book me a flight home mum. Aww, mum, you need to get me a flight".*

HOTEL WORKER: *"You must wait until the morning".*

NIECE: *"No, not tomorrow, Mum, I need to come back now".*

HOTEL WORKER*:* *"Now is not possible, tomorrow morning".*

(She is getting aggressive and stern again)

NIECE: *"Mum, please book me a flight now"!*

HOTEL WORKER: (Let me speak to your mum) *"Hello."*

NIECE: *"I wanna speak to her; I need to talk to her. I need to go home I can't stay here, I ain't got nowhere to stay, where am I gonna go until the morning."*

(The Hotel Worker hands back the phone)

NIECE: *"Mum, you need to book me a flight. I have not got anywhere to go.* (Crying) *I do not know where I am; please tell me where we are"* (talking to the hotel worker) please!"

(The Hotel Worker takes back the phone and speaks to her mum)

HOTEL WORKER: *"Hello, better you speak to you, your daughter… because she fights with her colleague, she a little bit drunk. She is in the room now, ok, don't worry."*

NIECE: (crying has stopped and personality change) *"Can you tell her to book me a flight, NOW, please. I can't stay here no more, I ain't got nowhere to go"!*

HOTEL WORKER: *"She go to bed and sleep and then leave tomorrow. It is better".*

NIECE: *"NO, no, can you please tell her... let me talk to her; please let me speak to her (starts crying again) Mum I need to come home today, don't listen to what he says please I need to come home. He is saying just wait until the morning, but I cannot wait till the morning I need to come home now. I do not know; I am going to have to walk mum. Oh please, I have not got anywhere else to go I am gonna be sleeping on the streets tonight, please, please book me a flight home. I just came back to get a coat (shouts) I come back to get a coat and apparently, I am a Loose Hoe because I came back to get a coat. (crying again) I just need to come home. Mum, Mum, please. I am begging you. I will give you the money; I will find the money. I'll give you money I just need to come home."*

NIECE: (to the Hotel worker). *"Please tell me where I am. Please tell me where I am."*

NIECE: *"How do you think I feel mum I haven't got anywhere to go? I am in a different country and I got nowhere to go (aggression) Pardons? She got out of bed to fight me, she got out of bed to fight me it was not the other way around, I did not attack her (stern but calm switch) She Got Out of Bed to Fight Me, It Was Not the Other Way Around (shouts at her mum) Because I Came into The Room to Get a Coat with My Friend, I said;* **"Ok I am gonna be out in a minute"***, she said hurry up before I box you down.*

I said wait I am getting my coat; I was trying to get a coat"... (crying again) Mum please can you book me a flight I need to come home right now (shouts with violent aggression) PLEASE BOOK ME A FLIGHT

HOME NOW MUM. *Mum please I am stuck here I will have to sleep on the street until Friday. Just get me a flight, please. Mum, mum I am gonna be stuck here until next week. Please, mum, I will find you the money. I will find you the money. Aunty Nicky, please tell me where I am so that I can get a flight home?"*

ME: *"I just sent your mum the details, so it is up to her what she does?"*

NIECE: *"She said she sent you details, she sent them to you already. Oh, mum, please I am stuck, I do not know I will walk to the airport Mum please I do not know what to do. Mum I haven't got anywhere to go unless you get me a flight home, Mum, Mum please (crying) mum please I am gonna move into the hostel, I'll pay you back, I'll pay you back for the flight, but I haven't got any way of getting home. What do you mean Mum I need you too what am I going to do, mum please, please I have not got anyone, and I have not got anywhere to go? I will; I will, I will please (shouts) I SAID I WILL, I WILL! So, what am I gonna do then, swim home, do not worry, do not worry, do not worry about it! Don't worry, man (switch) Don't worry about it, I am going, I am going now."*

(She puts down the phone and starts packing up her suitcase)

HOTEL WORKER: *"Come go to sleep, this your bed"* (pointing at the double bed)?

ME: *"No, she can sleep on that 1... single sofa-type bed."*

NIECE: *"Hello, Hello"*

(J, on the phone again to her mum in the background)

ME: (to hotel worker) *"You need to tell them cause I am not paying for her pulling the lamp out of the wall or the curtain,"*

NIECE: *"I need to come home. I'll pay for it; I'll pay for it, I'll pay for it mum I just need to come home, please"!!!*

HOTEL WORKER: *"She want to leave now?"*

ME: *"Hmmm"*

HOTEL WORKER: *"She want to go now?"*

ME: *"I don't know what she is doing."*

NIECE: *"I am going, don't worry... aww, I'll give it back to you. I will give it back to you Mum I just have not got anywhere else to go too; I cannot sleep on the streets for a whole week, I cannot stay on the streets until Friday. Why do you keep shouting when I have not done anything wrong? Do not worry, do not worry about it, just do not worry. I said do not worry about it (shouts) EXACTLY so do not worry.*

(her Mums voice heard on the phone)

B: *"I don't need this shit right now, J!"*

NIECE: *"Neither do I, yes; you do, yes, you do have a choice."*

ME: (to the Hotel worker) *"Apologies for this commotion."*

These are the five main things she mentioned which are complete lies and where she is 'chatting complete shit'.

- I did not get out the bed to fight her
- Never told her I would box her down
- She did not bring a coat with her on holiday
- I did not ask her to leave our room or go home
- It was between 18/20 degrees that night, warm as fuck. These were pure lies that came out of her mouth!

She was pleading with her mum to sort her out a flight to get home as she could not stay with me (remember) I did not tell her to go or leave the room that was her choice. I was not about to stop her as I was still getting my head around what had just taken place!!! Anyway, her mum says she will sort her out a flight which is when I tell her about the damages that her child has caused and that she would have to pay for it as I was not going to be paying!

My niece ends up leaving with the hotel worker and I remain in the room. I am in the bathroom washing my hands when I look in the mirror and cannot believe what I am seeing; the girl has attacked me like some fucking cat. My skin is 'redraw' with scratches and the flesh has been torn from my neck, face, arm and a little on my shoulder (joke business). She got her claws out because she wanted to mark up my fresh and clear skin! I return to bed a bit dazed and confused where the fuck did all that 'devil' behaviour came from; I am baffled!? How can she change so quickly like some devil child?

I replay the scene in my head, not that I want to, but my brain is on overdrive. The next day after the madness I am reluctant to step foot outside the hotel room as I could see people looking at my door as they walk past! Being as it is located right outside where all the sun-loungers are kept, and it is packed with people.

My thoughts were telling me

"They're waiting for you to open the door and walk out"

The drama last night was the top convo for some of the holidaymakers whether I liked it or not, that was the truth. I was far from a **'Lady in Control'** at this present time! More like a 'Lady in Hiding' instead, Lol! I felt so embarrassed and disappointed in her. So, here I am preparing myself to walk out the door, W.T.F.!!!

How was I feeling bad for what happened when it was not me who caused the drama? Confused.com - It was not about her attacking me my embarrassment and shame came from what she was shouting outside (that anyone awake would have heard) and if they were sleeping, they would have woken up. Kmt! The ultimate disrespect and degrading words that came out of her off-key mouth were all I was thinking about as those are not words of a 'right' minded person! In truth, she exposed herself to be one of those 'mixed race' people who is all for their 'Caucasian' side but quick to banish their black roots to fit in with the majority. Obviously, she does not acknowledge the blackness that she has in her, as she would **NEVER** have said what she did to me. Even as I am writing these words, I cannot believe what came out of her mouth. You honestly would not believe it unless you heard it. #Deep

For any moment, I have had in my life this was one that would have gone viral had I got to record or broadcast live on my phone. Finally, after a few hours of getting close to going out the door but then retreated a few times. The 'Lady in Control' returns, Lol. I left my room, full view to everyone with my head high, the red, raw broken skin in full view and went about my business! Ready and waiting for any questions (from people) that I had spoken to since arriving at the hotel. I was not going to allow this unbelievable drama to stop me from enjoying my 5* All-Inclusive, Crete, holiday. Hell, to The No! People came up to me asking

"Where's your friend?"

I was like she was not my friend she is my niece! Then when they saw my neck (not that you could miss it) then asked what happened, I told them that she was the person that scratched up my skin. They were all shocked!!! Even more so when I saw the 'couple' who we had been out with that same night were even more gobsmacked and could not believe what I was telling them.

Then they asked the same question everyone was asking.

"Why did she do it?"

A question I certainly do not know the answer too!!! I could have tried to cover up my neck, but it would have made no sense as I am in a hot country where many clothes are not needed. Now I have got these awful, flesh showing scratches that need to 'heal up quick' therefore I need the best natural remedy – the SUN! Nothing better than to have the sunray penetrate on all the marks so it can heal my skin, in no time, so that is what I did. I let it soak into my skin and whatever to those who saw my face and neck.

"It Is What It Is"

Simple! My life, my words, and my experience whose dramas, trials and tribulations have affected me, which has caused me to come across as abrupt, hard, and misunderstood at times; but won't allow any of it to 'BREAK ME'. I am stronger than I give myself credit for because being alone and not having anyone around (family) is what I adapted to years ago. I would rather remain this way than to be around toxic, red-eye, wicked and bad-minded people whether related or not! I know I am a genuine person with a heart of gold and yes, parts of me are still 'damaged goods' going through the healing process. Maybe one day, that will not be the case. #ImNotAshamed2AdmitIt

When I think about it, imagine if I had attacked one of my aunts on either of my parents' side, something I would never do! I cannot even imagine what they would think of me and I am sure they would never forgive me either as it is unforgivable. If you can be physically abusive to your mum (which she was) then attacking me was no biggie. Have I spoken or seen my niece, no I have not! Has she made contact to apologise, of course not!

But I do know since she has had two children, one being a girl who she lost due to being "still-born' in '2016 (I think!) something I would not wish on anyone.

Only God knows why he takes back the 'gift' of a child. R.I.P. to her daughter, my Great-Niece. x

Then in 2017/18, she was blessed with another child (boy) who I can only hope is being taken care of well and surrounded by love. Most of all I hope becoming a mother has made her a better person.

So, in reality, I am officially a great-aunt (twice) and love them both though I never got to meet and will probably never get to they are in my thoughts.

Do I think our relationship will get past this incident and be back in each other's life, anything is possible, but I do not see it happening and wish her all the best!

IF YOUR OWN NIECE

CAN ATTACK YOU

THEN SHE WAS NEVER

DESERVING OF YOU

Anikka Forbes

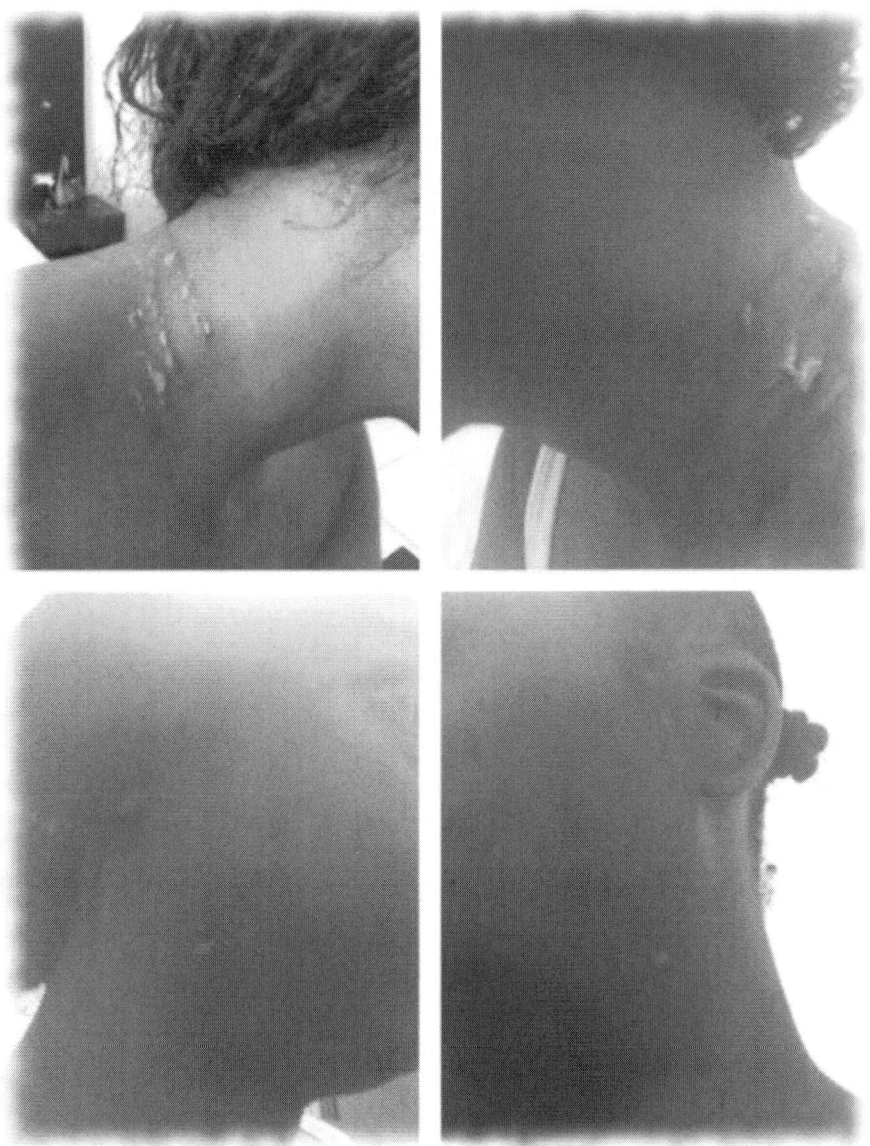

Photos taken a day after Niece attack!

Me and my Niece in November '2014

Me, Myself & I – After Attack!

CHAPTER 6: #TB 12 MONTHS

It's Monday 5th May '2014 at 00:09am, I have just finished ordering a belated birthday present for my niece J, a lovely 'D&G' watch. After having a reality check of myself that I had treated her in the same off-key, wicked, and hurtful way that my Aunt M had treated me back in '2010 when just like me, my niece was not to blame! Why! Because it was down to my brother (her Dad) to let me know I had a new niece on the way; though he was living up in wales and we were not in contact much. But I was in regular contact with J, who was the one who informed me, and she knew how upset I was about her Dad not bothering to tell me in the first place.

Then I was quick to cut her off then started talking to her like shit because I was even more disappointed and upset at her for not telling me her baby sister had arrived! Anyway, I have just un-blocked her on my Facebook account then sent her a message saying.

Just wanted to say, I am very sorry for being cold, wicked, and taking my hurt out on you regarding, your Dad. I do not expect you to accept my apology, but if I upset or hurt you; I am very SORRY!!! ☹ *I can say I am sorry as I know how I went on was wrong and realised I had treated you the same way as Aunt M treated me when I did not tell her about her husband's (affair) which was much worse, but the simple fact is YOU weren't to blame! But sometimes when you are feeling hurt, it can blind your vision and you say and do things which are not right, and this is one of those times!!! Your, my 1st niece and I LOVE you lots, always have and always will even though it was not evident over these last few months.*

You have a beautiful sister to be proud of and I am very proud and happy to have you both even if I do not see either of you much. It is one thing I can thank your Dad for, for having you! I will always be here for u and will never speak to you the way I did in my (last messages) again, as it was wrong. I do not want my relationship to be the way mine is with my Aunt (because I do care). Sorry I purposely ignored your 16th Birthday due to feeling hurt and upset (I will not) miss another again, wish you all the best in your exams and for the future.

Love you lots always and again I am very SORRY.

Aunty Nicky

I do not understand why I still feel so lost, confused, and lonely (no surprise). Honestly, I do not know what I am doing with my life other than working hard, putting myself forward for castings, trying to save and looking for somewhere to rent again by next month. Christian pisses me off (nothing new) because he has no consideration in letting me know whether were meeting up or not when he makes plans with me. Were meant to meet for some 'pub grub' but instead, his ignoring my calls! I tell myself

"I'm gonna lock him off"

Stop talking to him but I do not because I have accepted his 'letting-me-down' ways over these four years since knowing him, but it still does not make it right! The more I give him an inch; he takes a yard! I am one of the first people he calls to ask if he can borrow money (which is not a problem), though I am sure the term (borrow) means to lend and payback, but for him, it means to take, take, take, and never pay anything back or at least offer! Though I would never have accepted any money from him had it been the case, but it is just the courteous thing to do. My fault for allowing him to take my **'kindness for weakness'** though I will always help anyone IF I have the money. Yes, he is a good man with a heart of gold who is very funny and loves to make people smile and laugh (including myself), but it does not mean you take the fucking piss, knowing I have no one to rely on other than myself!

I could never ask him to lend me any as he never has money, which is why I have never refused him any because I believe you should **always help** if you can, those in need. I need to focus on me, getting my head and life right along with writing my first book. FFS (for fuck sake).

05.30 am just woken up, I look out the window and for the first time since working on this new project in Victoria (The Zig Zag Building), I do not want to go! Not because I am not enjoying it, trust me, I am! It is merely because I am in no rush to return to my desk to inhale the disgusting 🤢 **stench** smell of cheesy and moldy from a colleague's stinking foot/shoes.

The fact that he thinks I am making it up having practically said so last Thursday pissed me right off because if I were really a (bad-minded) person who did not care about other people's feelings, I would have told him there and then in front of the whole team. But I did not, though I am sure it would have shut him up! Instead, I have been biting my tongue, holding back while plenty others who also (smell) him, say nothing because they do not have to sit or work alongside him, but I do! So, I have decided I am not going in, or I will go in later; will decide after I (wake back up) again. At about 9 am, I receive a WhatsApp message from my (work colleague) worried at the thought of me not coming in today, so that is when I decide to get up. I wash, get dressed and leave out for work with my brain doing overtime, as it does.

I end up getting on the wrong train, bloody joker!!! So, by the time I get into work, it is after 11 am, she is so excited to see me (too cute) while stink foot is sat at his desk with his sour face, which I do not even pay any mind too. I sat down and got on with my work and did not say a word! Del (brother) sends me a text after 1 pm saying.

DEL: *"Nick can you call me if ur not busy"*

Does my brother want to ask me for money! So, I respond saying.

ME: *"I can't talk, so just text me whatever you have to say instead!"*

I continue with my work feeling so happy to have my beautiful niece 😊 back present in my life and cannot wait for her to receive her belated 16th Birthday present. I hope she likes it! We have been communicating throughout the day via FB Messenger and cannot believe when she tells me she is finished school already, only needs to go in for exams! Wow, how time has flown so quickly. Cannot even remember if that is how it was for me back then when I was going there, Lol! Cator Park School for Girls is what it was called back in the 90s, now it is called Harris Girls Academy. I received a call later that day from 'TAAS' (The Appropriate Adult Service) to cover a last-minute 'Contact Supervisor' shift tomorrow.

It has been about three years since I last did this job. Then I had Charmer WhatsApp a message offering me to visit him so he can give me his usual 'servicing' 😜. Then follows another WhatsApp message this time from Tamer, asking when we are meeting up, I responded saying

"you always ask then flop last minute".

It is now the early hours of the next morning at 03:16 am and I am sat in the living room feeling a little overwhelmed, but at the same time not surprised because I have 'consciously' been putting my wants, visions, and pictures on my wall of all I want to the universe for years.

The Secret (Law of Attraction) and confident that '2014, is my time for the big screen. Why, am I feeling so positive and sure because I was contacted via Skype by someone called 'Sarah Finn' a Top Casting Director from HOLLYWOOD plus an Actor, Director and Screenwriter called 'Jon Favreau' (googled their names) OMG! They told me they were contacting me about a film with Sylvester Stallone. It is the lead role they are casting for, it was offered to an Aussie lady, but she cannot do it anymore!!!

It is now 06:37 am and I have been awake from my 3hrs nap for about 30mins. Ben (flat mate) is deep-in-sleep, mashed (drunk) on the spare bed in my room and is <u>KILLING</u> me with his loud snoring, so I took myself down to the living room for a while! Now back in bed thinking about how long it is been since I started out trying to break into the world of acting in TV/Film, which was the year '2002. When LWT (London Weekend Television) was the ITV network franchise holder for Greater London and I participated in a documentary called **'Sex on the Job'** about having <u>sex</u> at work. I had this experience in my late teens, when I worked in retail with my ex-boyfriend, Lol. I am now in '2014, so that is a total of 12yrs. **12**, my significant number! I know God, Nan and the Universe is going to make this happen one day (by god's grace). Angela (medium) only a few weeks ago had asked about my acting and said to me.

"Don't Give Up, It Is Going to Happen."

While I am amending my niece's cv, I am also writing up the report from yesterday's 'Contact Supervisor' shift. Then receive a call from Christian saying,

CHRISTIAN: *"I just got out of a 3hr church service with my sister, I did some testimonies and will be going into Rehab".*

I responded,

ME: *"Is it? I have heard you say that many times before!"*

He tried to reassure me that he is serious this time and would see me soon! Low and behold at 7pm, there is a knock and one of the housemates opens the door, its him. He introduces himself to them with his crazy self, Lol!

Then he tells me he is hungry, so I make some food which we eat up in my room which is when I inform him about my unexpected skype casting convo last night from the USA, about the acting role. He is as excited as I am, but after telling him, I wished I had not, 😒 as he tells me not to get too excited due to past opportunities, I have mentioned, not working out as I had hoped, so true. I told him because were Bessie-mates, so regardless whether this opportunity is legit or not (fingers x) I have already opened my mouth!

Anyway, about an hour later, after he leaves, I return to my room and continue typing up the report. Then remember I need to take my clothes out of the washing machine, so I go downstairs, and Tony (another housemate) is in the kitchen, he asks

TONY: *"Have you spoken to Melissa"?*

I replied,

ME: *"I have not spoken to her in a while"*

Then he tells me they met up today, his face beaming with smiles which is when I tell him I think he is in love with her! During this year I nearly had a production created about me and it was going to be named after one of my alias names **'Bustylicious'**. A writer/friend Kofi Agyemang who I had worked with before back in '2009 in a sell-out Theatre Production called Strictly Bingo! Performed twice at Hackney Empire. He is the person who came up with the idea and it was going to be a mix of music, burlesque, and a great storyline.

Kofi's nephew an excellent dancer had started choreographing me, having had about two meetups but as much as I was excited and wanted to do it, I was not feeling good or confident within myself when it came to the dancing. Even though a few months before that I had done a six-week burlesque course, I even watched over and over the queen B (Beyoncé) sexy song 'Dance for You' trying to get inspired, but I felt like rubbish! I have not done dancing since my primary school years, which I loved and even won bronze and silver medals 🏅 but due to moving so much I never got to continue.

I know it would have been a fabulous production had I **'believed'** in myself and continued learning the routine etc. Thank you again, Kofi for presenting me with the opportunity and apologies for the disappointment. 🙍

Tuesday 13ᵗʰ May '2014: Well, it looks like I have been 'scammed' again this time via Skype from this so-called Sarah and Jon of HOLLYWOOD. From when the person asked me to <u>Get My Tits Out</u>, I knew they were playing games! Though I had done my research and believed those two people to be real; it turns out it was not them contacting me; instead, I had this sick, fake people **catfishing** me! But hey shit happens the main thing is I am safe, no harm done. Will try (hand over face) not to get caught out again. #GullibleMe

My niece messages me to say she is had a response back from a Modelling Company which offered her a free Photoshoot to help build up a portfolio and asked if I could call them on her behalf as they need to speak to an adult. I do my research on the company, then check out their site and all looks fine, so I call them to confirm that she wants to attend the shoot which is when they informed me a holding deposit of £50 is required. So, I pay it then they confirm her booking for Sat 24ᵗʰ and let me know an email will follow shortly.

I know that you should never pay any money upfront, but the £50 would be deducted of any photos that we decided to buy plus I knew she wanted to do the shoot, so paying was not an issue! I later get an email from the private renting company whom I am renting a shared-room with informing the household that there is a new flat-mate moving in and they will be room-sharing with me as of Friday!!! I pray that this newbie does not turn out to be off-key like the last two previous roommates but immediately go online to Flatland to check out other renting options (just in case). My head is feeling so confused.com not knowing if I want to continue room-sharing as it is cheap living. While hoping I will be able to save more but on the other hand, it is not always easy living with strangers, let alone sharing a room with one.

So, fingers and toes crossed all will be fine. I ended up going to meet with Christian for some pub grub and a catch up. End up having a smoke, having not smoked in about three months though feeling a little guilty but after the way, I was feeling vexed, I needed it! While we were chatting, I received a call from my (Agent) Jack asking if I was free on Monday for a Music Video job, I told him yes and that's when he tells me there is NO audition, I have already been selected to do it! Bloody hell, that is a first! Thank you, Jack.

He emails me over the details. As mentioned in Chapter 4 it was for the artist Passenger aka Michael David Rosenberg, to play the role as an Office Person.

Saturday 17th May '2014: It is just after 3pm when I receive a WhatsApp message from Charmer asking.

> *"Are you busy. Do you want a (servicing)?"*

I tell him I am at work so would let him know later though I am in two minds but could so do with his service. Lol! I get home at about 6pm, chillaxed while still deciding whether to go to Charmers. Then before 21:00, another WhatsApp from him pleading with me too,

> *"Bring my sexy ass to him as he is so horny."*

So, I decided to go, left out and drove down to Barbican by 10pm. As I approach his door, there he is waiting to greet me with open arms (it is always) great to see him. Were sat down for about 5mins then he wants to pop out to the shop. We get back from the shop, start talking, have a little smoke, some jokes and then he takes off my shoes then starts massaging my feet, but they smell a little (cheesy) to me, so I ask him if I can borrow a towel to wash my feet. Then he suggests for us to share a bath, so we do! But boi, all I can say (LMFAO) I **never** expected ever to witness seeing what was presented to me by him, I am already in the bath when he comes in with a 'black lacy thong' on telling me,

CHARMER: *"It is my fetish wearing women's knickers",*

and I responded.

ME: *"Hey, it is each to their own and if that's your thing… then who am I to judge?"*

It is funny I know for a fact and can always tell with him by his eyes, the change in the way he speaks (over-talking), a little sweaty and then follows the stripping off naked indicates his on a high. Having popped out of the living room to go and have some 'cocaine'. It was one of those times except this time he felt confident/brazen enough to wanna share with me his **'knicker'** fetish! We have a little soak, get out the bath then he gives me a lovely rub down with the body lotion and then starts worshipping my feet/toes (don't know why he loves them off so much), but I am certainly not complaining. Then he lays me back to indulge in his usual on-point and fabulous servicing (oral) pleasure only! No physical as it ain't about that anymore; but he still wants to 'eat' which is guaranteed satisfaction every time!

Sunday 25th May '2014: What a day it is been today, my niece and I wake up at 07:30am, something tells me to look out the window, so I do! Why am I staring at a car that looks like the one I had parked around the back last night!!! So, I get the car key, press the open button to see if it is the car (it is) I nearly pass out! WTF, confused.com! - Did someone steal it, go for a joy ride, then return it to that spot? Crazy, but it is the only explanation I can think of and anything is possible. I call the rental company to see what they had to say, ready and waiting to get in trouble.

This response is what they said to me.

> *"You were obstructing the driveway.*
> *We had been trying to call you but had no luck!*
> *So, we called the police, then the*
> *removal people who then moved the car."*

OMG, J, and I could not stop laughing! Though it was not a laughing matter and I am sure (zipcar) was far from impressed. Had my phone not died I would have received their call, trust it to be me to cause such inconvenience. Kmt!!! Anyway, we end up driving down the road to drop it off then head to the Gym/Spa at VA in Chiswick. It is lovely having J's company; we have a workout then go to relax in the spa area for about an hour, later we have a race in the pool together, which is Nuff jokes. Quality time with her, love it!

We take a few 'selfies' after we get dressed then it is straight to Argos in Hammersmith as I want to get a little speaker for my iPhone, but instead I end up getting the CD attachment for my laptop so I will be able to send J's Modelling pics to her when they arrive in the post.

Then I ask her to pick where we should go to eat, but she cannot decide, so we nearly settle for a salad from Subway until as were walking through Hammersmith Mall I remember the lovely pub that I had visited over the last few weeks which does lovely sweet potato fries, so we go there to eat instead.

While we were eating, I received a WhatsApp message from an unknown number saying.

UNKNOWN: *"Nikz, u ok."*

I responded:

ME: *"You are"*

The person replied:

UNKNOWN: *"Hmmm, TD"*

I do not answer! Fed up with these guys that think they can go quiet for months on end and then suddenly make contact. KMT! Christian calls my phone. I was not going to answer, but I did! He is complaining saying.

"Why haven't you called me."

When he knows full well, he had his phone switched off! I tell him where I am down the road from his home with my niece, so he pops along to join us for a while, making us laugh as he does as you can never stay mad at the joker for too long!

Then he gets a call from his sister asking why he is not at church! So, we decide to all leave together; we walk over to the bus stop and all jump on the bus up to Fulham, Christian gets off two stops before us. When I get home, it is straight up to my room to lay down due to not feeling too well!

J asks if I mind her going outside to have a Smoke😶, then 30mins later she comes up to my room to tell me she is heading home, so we hug, I give her a big kiss then I walk her to the door. Never in a million years would I have believed that a year later, my niece would have verbally and physically attacked me. FAMILY, as proven, can also be your worst enemy and your biggest disappointment, but we live, and we learn!

I am grateful for the memories, photos, and footage that I have of her or us which I will always cherish! And just for the record, I do not care if your family, friend, or foe.

If your fake, off-key or full of negativity and do not have my best interest at heart.

"YA GOTS TO GO."

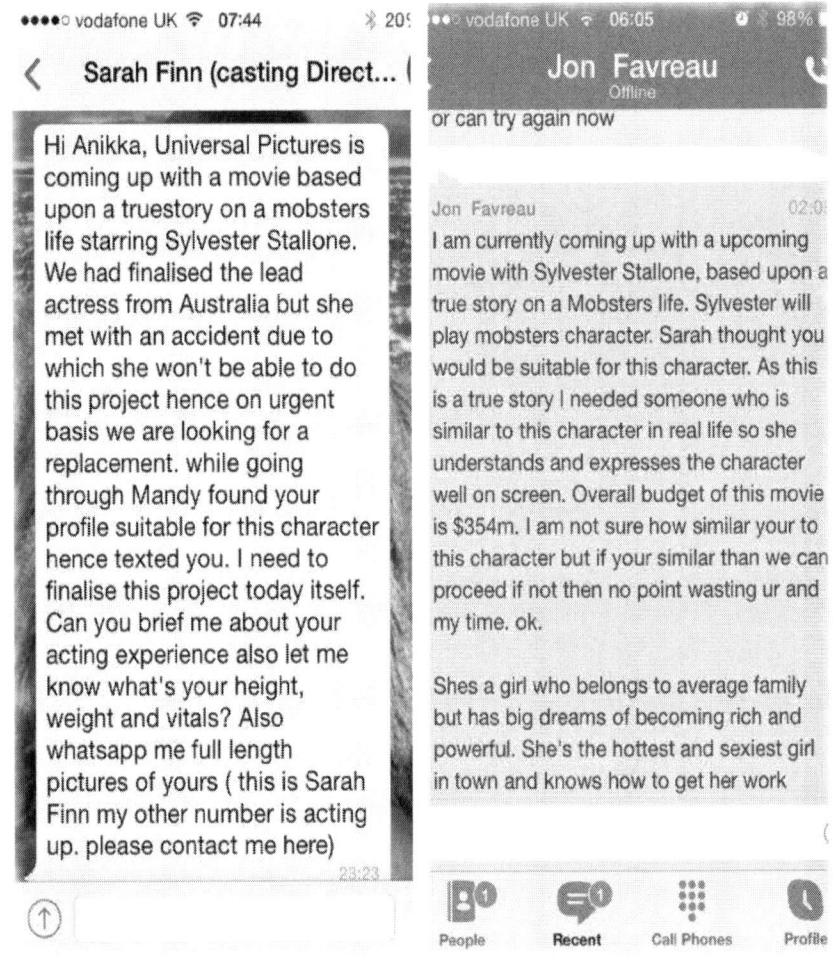

Skype: Catfishing Messages

DON'T FEAR THE ENEMY

THAT ATTACKS YOU

BUT THE FAKE FRIEND

WHO HUGS YOU?

UNKNOWN

CHAPTER 7: SERTRALINE vs SEROTONIN

DEPRESSION. Just the sound of the word conjures up images most want to avoid or ignore. But guess what? Depression is as real as it sounds and does not discriminate when it hits! For whatever reason, it is something that many people (if you admit) to suffering from it are dealing with it daily. Some cannot function at all in life as everyone's experience is different! I am not minimising the extent of depression, but as someone who has struggled with it most of their life, it is not easy! I can tell you from my experience it is something I would not wish on anyone. For the simple fact that as seen on the (news), it can cause people to take their own life! Though this is nothing new.

The reality is people of the world have been suffering from mental health for a lifetime. But the truth is due to certain people of the celebrity world sharing their experience; it has become top priority. And now EVERYONE seems to be making claims to suffering from depression to sell a story or get sympathy! #justsaying

Do not get me wrong I am glad it is now highlighted everywhere you look and taken seriously with more knowledge and help available to the genuine ones. It can be manageable although it takes a hell of a lot of work, self-care and sometimes medication. There has always been a negative stigma attached to the subject of mental health. The words 'mad and crazy' is what I recall hearing from my younger days, where my older brothers Dad was concerned due to him being a patient at the well-known Maudsley Hospital in Denmark Hill. My older brother often had the words.

"You're sick in the head like ur Dad"

Said to him by Mum, Nan, and Uncle. Mental abuse is what this is! I know for sure it has affected him till this day because I witnessed them say it many times as a child. My brother is four years older than me, born in '1977 and we both have different Dads though he always referred to my Dad as his own. As a child, I did not like him calling him Dad, because as far as I was concerned, he had his Dad and I had mine. Dad referred to him as his son which in all honesty was rightly so because my brother was present in my parents' life before I came along, but as a child, I did not see it like this!

Do I know much about his father (not really) only what I heard come from family members mouths?

"He is a mad man who went off his head and in and out of Maudsley hospital".

An upsetting memory which my brother recalls from his childhood which he has mentioned to me a few times over the years, I would say it was a form of mental abuse because it is something that has stayed with him all his life and has impacted on his mental state. He recalls a time as a child in the early eighties when he was out in the car with our uncle and aunty driving and they spotted his Dad and they said to him.

"Look Del, there's your mad Dad"

They both started laughing! How wicked and cruel is that!? Who does that please! You certainly would not expect it to be your aunt and uncle, but they were laughing at the father of their nephew who suffered from mental health problems. Can you imagine how he felt or how you would feel hearing these words as a child from two (grown-arse adults) who should have known better! Instead, they were humiliating and hurting his feelings not realising that what they did would stick in his head forever; it is heart-breaking just thinking about it even now. I feel bad knowing that sometimes whenever my brother and I would argue or fight, I would repeat to him out of spite

"You're mad like your Dad"

Without knowing what I was saying. But that is what innocent children do, they copy what they grow up around hearing and that was no different for me and certainly does not make it right. I am so sorry from the bottom of my heart – for any hurt I may have caused you back then. x

Mental Health was/is something; people believed they should be ashamed to admit or even talk about to anyone. There are different degrees of depression and it can target any one of us, at any time. But most of all, it is something that you may encounter at some point depending on your life experiences! For those with a healthy support system around them, they can sometimes get through their depression without any problems!

Unfortunately, many do not have any support, so end up getting lost forever with **'no light at the end of the tunnel'** only more and more darkness. There is a variety of depression that people can experience, maybe more and they are Atypical depression, Major depression, Persistent depression, Psychotic depression, Postnatal depression, Seasonal depression, and Situational depression.

These are also some of the common symptoms that may have occurred at some point in a person's life, but never had a clue that it was signs of depression! Deep feelings of sadness, dark moods, feelings of worthlessness or hopelessness. Your appetite and sleep changes, lack of energy, inability to concentrate, difficulty in getting through your normal activities. A lack of interest in things you used to enjoy, withdrawn from family and friends, preoccupation with death or thoughts of self-harm. To the point where some see no way out, so 'take their own life. #sadbuttrue

There is a level of depression that is so debilitating that it can leave a person unable to function. Schizophrenia is something characterised by abnormal social behaviour and failure to understand what is real. Common symptoms include false beliefs, unclear or confused thinking, hearing voices that others do not hear. Reduced social engagement and emotional expression plus a lack of motivation. In some cases, it results in a person being locked away behind closed doors within a hospital, segregated from the world while under twenty-four-hour watch. They can even be injected with medication to help calm them down or put in a straitjacket if deemed to be a **'danger to themselves or others**.

All depending on the type of mental health disorder, they are suffering from, which affects one in four people in any given year. It is interesting now to see how much its discussed in the news, on television and within the Entertainment Industry. I think mental health has become more of a serious topic of discussion because of people in the public eye!

They are no longer hiding the fact that it is real and regardless of status, it can affect anyone down to children before the start of teenage years. Mothers who suffer from it after giving birth, are now being taken seriously when they feel their suffering from postnatal depression. The symptoms include feeling down and teary, an inability to concentrate, low sex drive, to name a few!

The truth of the matter is, we can all suffer from depression at some point in our life as it comes in many forms and affects people differently! In big or small doses and can bring a person to the lowest or profound feeling you could ever imagine to where they end up committing suicide. Trying to commit suicide is something that no one can ever imagine unless your someone who has tried and failed! My belief is (it was not) their time to die, which is why they survived to live another day. I know about depression! Because as hard as it is for me to write this knowing that I am exposing the only genuinely dark treasured secret to you, the reader, family, friends, and associates.

I confess depression IS something that identifies with me too well and now laying it bare to you all to read! I believe in being authentic and it would not be genuine of me to write this book without sharing this part of my life. Thank god within the last 2-3years much needed help and support finally came my way. #betterlatethannever

I have never tried to commit suicide. But yes, there have been a few times the thought of *'taking my own life'* had crossed my mind during the dark, lonely, and unworthy periods! The feeling of not wanting to exist anymore! To wishing that my mum had 'terminated' me when she had the chance as neither of my parents made me feel like I was someone's child. Depression is a part of me; it has been for many years! Healing and managing it is easier to accept when you admit to yourself that you suffer from it. Therefore, it is a part of your life, whether you like it or not!

When you are in denial about it, that is when the suffering in silence can become unbearable. And yes, I have known for years but chose to keep it to myself! Why because though I am an open book, I am reserved with the deep inner me. Never been one who offloads feelings or emotions onto anyone other than expressing all in my diaries. I know for a fact that God brought Dad and me back together when he saw the time was right! We are both older, wiser and in need of finally having the father and daughter bond, from all the years missed prior. Not long after reuniting I remember he said to me.

"Princess, I can see the sparkle in your eyes is missing."

His words, having just been back in my life five-minutes! He saw what no one else could (straight through-me) which goes to prove regardless of his absence; he knows his child. That moment he educated me about

'Serotonin', something I had never heard about until then and this is what he believed to be missing. **Serotonin** is a chemical nerve that cells produce. Serotonin in the brain is thought to regulate anxiety, happiness, and moods. Low levels of the chemical have been associated with depression and increased serotonin levels brought on by medication are thought to decrease arousal. I finally put my *"I am fine and don't need no help"* stubbornness behind me. So visited my doctor to enquire about my Dad's concerns for me, my brain and well-being. The moment I started talking, he handed me a questionnaire to fill out (which I did not expect) and the questions varied from.

- Feeling worthless
- Oversleeping or not sleeping
- Thinking you would be better of not being here

On one or two questions, I had marked two answers, but the doctor told me I could only pick one! I could see in his face that he was surprised with my answers and how long I had been coping alone! He started checking my notes though I explained I had (never) spoken about it before. Though I was aware, I suppose I was in denial too! So just wanted to keep it to myself, like I have all these years. The Doctor then asked me a few more questions from another form. Which is when he told me I was suffering from **'moderate, severe depression'**.

The depression part I already knew! I just never had it confirmed before nor given an official name until now. **Depression** is a mood disorder characterised by irritability or depressed mood and lack of interest in once pleasurable activities. It can be mild, moderate, or severe. Only **severe** cases warrant a diagnosis of major depression which is treated using psychotherapy, medication, and exercise.

Friday 16th October '2015: Is when I had the doctor's appointment and then collected my first Sertraline prescription tablets from the chemist. I could feel my brain going to work, slowly but surely regaining the lost serotonin. Sertraline is an antidepressant of the selective serotonin reuptake inhibitor class. It was introduced to the market by Pfizer in 1991. It helps many people recover from depression and it has fewer unwanted effects than older antidepressants. I believe my 'depression' started before my teens as I cried a 'hell of a lot' when alone out of sight from anyone seeing!

In my early twenties, after being involved in a fatal car accident which impacted on my mind more than I knew until referred to counselling. Every session, I would break down into tears while also expressing my feelings from my upbringing. I now see that both my Nan and mum were emotionally and physically damaged goods too who were unable to properly build me up in the way needed, for every young girl child, boy or nonbinary. Though I was still a little reluctant to take the daily sertraline tablet, I did take them!

I could feel the positive change from the Medaric brand that I was taking; my brain just felt happier. Until eleven months later, on 16th September '2016 when it came to re-ordering my prescription. The chemist informed me that the 'brand' I had been using for the last eleven months had now been discontinued and so they sent me a brand called Accord. This new brand was not like the other and though the chemist tried to reassure me that it was the (same) I thought; ***"Err, hello".*** How can anyone (professional or not) tell me how I feel when straight away, I noticed a difference! I went for nearly a year on a high, happy, and positive.

To suddenly feeling the way, I use to at times, i.e., super low, moody, and wanting to stay in bed sleeping rather than wake-up and face reality. So, I stopped taking them for about a week or two until another brand was given to me to try! Boi, the side effects (while waiting) had me dizzy, with headaches, off-balance and my mood at times were so vile that I did not even like myself, it was terrible! All from just stopping instead of gradually coming off it. Three years and three months, I tried and then at the beginning of '2019 I decided I was going to stop taking the sertraline.

Why because the brand had changed four times and the lows had returned, which was not a good thing! Most of all, I wanted to take back control by dealing with the depression phases - like I always did prior by (just getting on with it) without taking pills. I should have weaned myself off slowly, but I did not! I do not recommend anyone doing the same as I did!

The brain is not something to mess with and though I did not stop correctly, thank god I am alright! As mentioned before, I know depression is part of me, but I refuse to allow myself to be dependent on any medication! I managed years before it so will continue to cope now that I have stopped taking the different brands of Sertraline. Where am I now with my state of mind in 2019. Well, I can honestly say this year had me up and down with my thoughts and emotions. So much so that back in June again, I felt like I no longer wanted to be alive anymore! I have been feeling lost with my life, not knowing what I am doing anymore, no partner or kids.

To missing and worrying about my Dad plus disappointed and hurt with him 'ghosting' me all over again like most of my life; with no contact for most of 2018. Only seen him once this year which was on my birthday, apart from that nothing! Then reflecting on the past few years and asking myself
"Why God made my parents have me!"

It is all a mixture of how the negative depression (devil) creeps in and attacks my mind. Until I snap out of it and tell myself to fix-up and think positive.

Monday 17th June '2019: A week before starting my first official SIA Security job within construction, I was on a severe downer. A poem created from this dark moment which I decided to share via my blog on my website; instead of keeping it to myself as I would typically do! I named it.

WOULD U BELIEVE ME?

It is deep!
I do not know what I am doing with myself or life anymore

Once again, I am at that lower than low
Where I wanna just lock the door

See what is on the other side.

What is going on in my head to make me feel like this

I know I need to fix-up and snap out of it, but it will not shift
It is me, myself, and I

My brain is thinking about all sorts
I am tired with life

Nothing to show for it
I was not meant to be born

So why am I here
I thought I knew my purpose

Yet I feel so worthless
Would you believe me

If I told you I broke down and cried today

Thank god I am out of unemployment and back working,

Keeping Busy and Making Money

Is a motto I used as a Document Controller of twelve years, making great money! Now I am currently doing security, the money does not even touch what I was earning as a DC, but it is not about the money; instead, it is about no longer feeling restricted to an office but being free and trying something new until I work out what I want to do next.

While still in search of happiness and can only hope one day, it will come my way by God's grace. Amen

"There IS Hope, Even

When Your Brain Tells

You There Isn't."

John Green

CHAPTER 8: UP, CLOSE & PERSONAL

I think most females who are attracted to men hope that one day they will find their Mr Right or like the fairy tales which has a prince charming, looking for his princess, like myself! Lol - I was born and raised in the West where arranged marriages are not immensely popular unless within specific cultures, which I do not agree with, but everyone is different!

I have had my fair share of dates, mingles and on and off relationships with men of different races, heights, and ethnicities because I am a real **L.O.V (Lady of Variety)** with no issue about age either, as we all know it is just a number! This path of discovering who I am not only as a Black Nubian Lady in Europe but one who has ancestry that traces back several centuries to an African Royal Bloodline. I have come to realise that people become who they are for many reasons; one of which is without a doubt their upbringing.

I have no regrets for any of the privileged men who have been lucky to either date or get 'up, close and personal' with me as they were all meant to be a part of my life regardless of the length of time! As the saying goes.

> *"Not everyone is brought into your life to stay some are just passing through."*

Here's an example - we all want to find someone that is honest, loyal, caring, and hardworking but due to past let-downs your subconscious mind continues to focus on the negative from past relationships instead of focusing on the positives and all you want, so you end up only getting the 'I do not want' type. Therefore, you must change your mindset, know you're worth, but most of all remember you can do **"bad by yourself"** without any man, woman or LGBTQ in your life who is NOT worthy of you! #NoteToSelf

Soon after returning from Crete and dealing with the craziness of my off-key niece, I began watching 'The Secret' again non-stop and re-embracing the 'Law of Attraction'. I figured that maybe I had been drawing everything negative and off-key into my life based upon what I had been writing in my diaries over the last 16years. Simply because I do not leave anything out when I write about my daily life; good or bad! Yes, that includes the men that have passed through my life! That day forward, I had decided that I would NO LONGER write about anything negative and if so, then turn it around into a positive!!! Today, I always say that I am happy, healthy, able, and financially stable with the first two being the most important!

One day I hope I will have my secure roof over my head! I want to continue drawing nothing but positivity into my life along with any life-changing, great opportunities that may come my way, as of now 2017 onwards. No more negativity being written in my diaries as it is officially the weakest link. LMFAO!!!

Before I got to that state of mind, I had to go through some tough lessons about love. First and foremost, until you love yourself completely, you leave little to no room to be loved by someone else the right way. Having a positive image about yourself (instead of what others think) and learning how to convey that in your attitude plus behaviour can make a world of difference.

Some people think I am either too direct or outspoken whereas I see it as me simply being a **realist** who says how I see it, without holding back at times but never trying to be disrespectful or hurtful. I know from experience my words can cut as deep as a knife simply because I write exactly the way I think and talk in detail! I have offended many along the way, with my harsh and very stubborn self. But we are all entitled to our own opinion, sometimes you must be cruel to be kind or turn and walk away!

Yes, like most I want to find 'the one', fall in love, marry (if not) that is fine too and have children, but this chapter in my life, has not yet arrived. Then, on the other hand, I have always been so driven by wanting a career within the Entertainment Industry while continuing to write my diaries and hoping to meet that 'special someone' who will love me and soften me as I know my hard/cold ways at times is a working progress!

For one reason or another, my life has been more work than play with the male side of things being a mixture of good times along with some very draining encounters which is why the **"single and free to mingle"** has worked best for me. There is no such thing as "perfect' nor is that something I am looking for either. All I want is to be loved unconditionally and love back the same because we all deserve that. I will continue to grow and become the best version of myself for me to attract the best version of a man who I will ultimately share a great future with and who will be the father of my future children, if I am blessed with any! #IHope

One hundred per cent I can relate to what they say about female Capricorns. Yes, I am *'down to earth, self-motivated, patient and responsible with some personality traits which often confuse partners in the early stages of a relationship. I admire those who are hard-working or have ambition and little tolerance for lazy people, give me the company of optimists over pessimists any day'.* Though I can be a mix between both, sometimes!

I have always got along better with the opposite sex, which is baffling being as both times during my Primary School years I was bullied, by boys! But in all honesty, men have never phased me. I remember back when I was between the ages of 7-10, I was staying with my god-sister

Tracey down in Deptford, as that was one place that I loved going to at the weekends or during school holidays because it was always guaranteed fun. Her Dad a top-class man whose cooking I could not get enough off! Mr West was the first man that I (told off) in defence of my god-sister whenever I felt he was too hard on her. Once I let my little mouth go too far because he ended up telling my mum and aunts, so I got in trouble! What can I say, my mouth was too much from then! Then there is the Construction Industry a male-dominated world that I have been contracting in for the last twelve years and it will chew-up and spit-out any female who is timid, quiet and cannot hold her own!

That is not me! Anyone who has worked with me would agree. I am naturally a dominate lady who can fit in like one of the lads, because I am not bothered by the swearing, antics, or those few who either think their 'shit don't stink' or that females are below them! It is all good and I love it. Some men can be intimidated by a strong-headed female (like myself) what can I say,

"I am my father's child"

He embedded in me from a young age to respect myself, never allow a man to put his hand on me and not to be afraid of no one only the creator! I was briefly seeing a guy who I referred to as TD aka 'Turkish Delight'. We met in May '2011 when he messaged me via FB Messenger for the first time on my 1 of 2, Facebook profiles; Nicky (Ms USB) ultra, sexy, babe. He loved my modelling pics and wanted to let me know! TD was in his late twenties, cheeky, fun, VERY sexy and naughty but nice, is what he was to me! He was the sweetest guy as I got to know him, but I began to see a pattern although he would reach out to me through calls, texts, or messenger. But there were times where he would disappear on me for months then appear again.

I learned a few weeks later that TD's past had some crime elements to it which had landed him in prison. Regardless, I still cared a lot about him and although he tried his best to stay out of trouble, he ended up back in jail only a few weeks of our meeting. Then I heard nothing from him until out of the blue on Saturday 27th April '2013. I got up just after 10:00am having just finished eating the other half of a nasty takeaway; could not have been that (nasty) as I still ate it. Lol! Anyway, I received a phone call message from an automotive system that I had been getting all week on both mobiles but thought nothing of it. I was just about to cut off the phone when I heard,

"Someone is trying to contact u from HMP Prison"

Straight away, I wondered who that would be! The only person I could think was TD, so I accepted the call, and it was him. So, shocked, but at the same time I was happy, it was nice to hear from him because no matter what he always found a way to contact me to see if I was ok. I will never forget and will always be grateful for when he sent me a message from prison back on Thursday 2nd Feb '2012 the day of my Nans funeral to let me know while locked up behind bars that he was thinking of me.

It is the little things that mean the most to me and that memory will always be treasured. TD called to see how I was, then when I asked how he was doing he told me that he was finishing off his probation with seven months left then it would be all over after eight years from when it all started. I told him that he had confused the hell out of me as to why he still cared and kept in contact. I asked him why he keeps returning into my life; Here is his response.

TD: *"I know it is true; you've always been there for me since we met on Facebook back in '2011. I don't know Nik, you just got me like that, always coming back!"*

Then he told me they had moved him to a new prison in Thamesmead called Thameside. I told him I would always have time for him, no matter what! I liked him a lot and though I am sure it would have been challenging it would have been great for us to have had something serious, but it was not meant to be so remaining friends aka 'fuck-buddies' was all good. I still stayed in touch with him while he was serving his last few months, even sent him some money from time to time. I will always help anyone if I can! #StandardProcedure

Then back in Feb '2014 when I was living in Chiswick, W4 my fourth postcode move since relocating to West London. I had just got out of the spa and into the changing rooms at VA Gym when I looked on my phone and saw a text from an unknown number which said.

MESSAGE: *"Yo! Ms Fine as Wine"*

A big smile appeared on my face, straight away, I thought there is only one person who calls me that, TD. 😊

ME: *"How are you, stranger."*

He later responds.

TD: *"Hey babe sorry replying now, only just got my phone and it was on charge! Anywayz I have been good, now that jail time is behind me. How you been?"*

ME: *"Hey, no probes Hun. Was an unexpected, pleasant surprise to see your text you know how we do! But all is good it is a new year, a new chapter and glad to hear your jail time is behind you. Hope 2014 onwards is blessed 4u."* 🌿

His last reply was.

TD: *"Lol, no doubt it is good to know you're ok doe"* :o)

It was lovely of him to make contact again and I love it when he refers to me as Ms. Fine as Wine. Was he hoping I was going to suggest we meet up, although I wanted to see him again, my stubbornness was not prepared to entertain longness (time-wasting) anymore or allow my emotions to get messed with again! Although I enjoyed our few weeks of spending time together and the great sex, it was not enough and I deserved more because no matter who your intimate with, date or find attractive you must look at that relationship through the lens of truth and future. I remember doing my research on him out of curiosity, as I now knew his full name but (not expecting) to find anything. Surprisingly, I did! Why am I looking at his face, clear as day on a local newspaper website with the words?

Police hunt man recalled to prison serving part of an eight-year sentence for aggravated burglary'.

Some would say that I should have cut him off as soon as I found out he was back in jail or saw the newspaper article, but for me, that is not a good enough reason to kick someone out of my life whose done me no harm. #RealTalk

I do not agree with any crime, but there are far worse people in the world who have committed unlawful and perverted crimes, none of which relate to TD. I got to know a side of him that was loving, kind and vulnerable. He kept his street life separate away from me. Yes, he was good-looking, charming, and damn fine. But I did not know much about him and neither was I looking for one of those relationships where the guy was known by police, therefore the likelihood of him being sent back to prison for whatever reason, for me was a definite no, no! On the other hand, I have spent most of my life on my own, so having a man inside probably would not have been hard for me to deal with as I adapt well to situations.

I am like a light switch, once I turn off there is no going back and if you are lucky to creep back in, I cannot guarantee a third time lucky! For me, it is all about moving forward because I know my worth and I would rather be (single and free to mingle) until God is ready to deliver my man, future husband, and father to my child/ren to me. Amen

May 2017, my heart was saddened, shocked, and hurt to find out via the same place we first met Facebook, that TD had died in an accident doing what he loved, riding his motorbike. Even as I am writing this, I still cannot believe he is gone! I will always cherish the short quality time spent with him and at least I will always have something to remind me of him, his cherished letters; Here is one of the letters he wrote me from prison back in 2013.

19.06.2013

Hey Nicks

Hi, do not know where to start I am not in that prison in London. Since then, I have been moved to 3 other prisons. The day I got moved, I refused, but they rushed me away. They left all my stuff behind and to top it off where that prison was privately run the pin phone systems are totally different to government ones, so you had to register all over again.

Well, I ain't got no number like I said the basterds left everything behind. You sent me a few emails I have just got them recently instead of sending them, i.e. Forwarding them on to me they have kept them at Thameside till it is all stacked up, by the way, thank Q for my B'day card put a big smile on my face. 😊

Anyways love the pic yeaaa boy Miss Fine as Wine yea, SNM (say no more) I see you. X

Well like I was saying, so they forwarded your letters to Wayland then they forwarded it onto Highpoint North, then to Highpoint South joke ain't even the word! Anywayz at the moment I am stressed out differently right now, down the Block (long story) I am

trying to stay out of trouble, but it always seems to find me and on top of that the governors 'shall I say' gave me 28days loss of everything no canteen, no phone, credit... mad but you know what I'm ma ride it like I always do if I do two months down seg I have got another 2mths left right now it is what it is, ya see it!

Moving on your emails Nicks what was all that about Hmmmmm, no comment! Well, I was not blanking you for a start, but I understand why you would think like that! Anywayz how's life outside in the real world not really been much of a summer has it. Well, the more grey cloud,
the better for me. Lol

Did you hear back from your interview? Anywayz Nicks sorry if I keep going on cannot wait to get out of this shit hole, this human money-making trap I was doing good in Thameside since then lost a fair bit of weight, stress!!! Anywayz sorry about my messy handwriting I tend to write like this when stressed and mad, lol.

Well just make sure you look after yourself Miss Fine as Wine.

LOVE + HUGS and KISSES.
TD. xx

TD was a 'want' that was not to be long term in my life. I appreciate the time we shared; may he rest in peace. My life has moved on and I have met other men who have continued to help me know **'what I do and don't want'** as a partner or future potential husband.

July '2014, I dated a twenty-seven-year-old Pakistani man, named Ali for six months when I was living in Fulham working on the 'Zig Zag Building' project in Victoria, London. He was one of the security guards on-site, I remember when I first laid eyes on him his pretty striking features, for a man, was captivating. So sweet and lovely with an innocent nature with a little to no experience when it came to relationships and that was confirmed when he told me he was a virgin! That did not put me off if anything it was cute and I fell for his adorable personality, deep spiritual side not his experience as I was more than happy to be his teacher, Lol.

I remember just two weeks of us getting to know each other I was at home not feeling too well while he was at work on one of the sites, but he wanted to come and take care of me. I genuinely hoped and believed that he was the one for me, we spoke about marriage, having kids and going to meet his family in Pakistan. I trusted and opened my heart up to him and he could read me more profound than any man I had ever met due to his amazing spiritual connection. I had spoken on numerous occasions via skype to his brother and sister back home.

But his family wanted him to get married, ideally, an arranged marriage which he told me he would not do as it was his choice to find his wife. 95% of our quality time was me driving to keep his company during his night shifts between the two sites that he was working on in Waterloo and Battersea. I worked in the day as a Document Controller and he worked at night as Security; therefore, I was the only one who could make the journey to him having not long got a new car so getting about was no issue.
I did not mind at all because when you miss someone, you will make time, so as long as I got to spend time with him, that was better than nothing!

I would bring a quilt, pillow, and my fan heater so that we would be cosy for the couple hours we got to spend together daily. Did we have sex, yes, we did, did I take his virginity? I suppose (if) he was a virgin!

To cut a long story short, I later found out that while Ali had returned home for a visit to see his poorly father a trip I was (meant) to join him on he had gone alone and done what he said he would not do, an arranged marriage! As you can imagine, this was not the news, I was expecting to hear, but in the back of my mind, I had foreseen something like this happening! Maybe he got there and had no choice plus being a respectable, family orientated person whose belief and faith in God was a big deal for him even more so being Muslim; he regularly prayed throughout the day. I honestly could not see him ever saying no to his family's request even more so as it had only been a few years prior since his mum died which had affected him tremendously, so much that I had seen him shed a few tears in the few months we were together.

I tried to confront him, which ideally would have been better face to face but had to make do with texting and as expected, he denied it! I tried calling him, but he was not returning my calls just messaging me, then had the cheek to return from Pakistan to London after six weeks and did not bother telling me he was back! This hurt because I honestly believed it was the start of something great, but as the saying goes

"Actions speak louder than words".

If you are wondering how I found out that he had married, I was told by the Astrologer who was on-point about so many things in my life I had no reason not to believe her and the proof was in the pudding! I decided to block him, so no more calls or texts but then unblocked him a few months later. We have since communicated with each other briefly via text only because I have moved on from the hurt and disappointment; I had regarding him. I have no reason to stop speaking to him now, even though things did not work out, I wish him all the best in his future.

*"When you can move on from heartache
with no regrets, you have healed."*

Then there was Ed, a sixty-two-year-old Brazilian who declared his undying love for me within two days of us meeting back in May '2015. There I was not long back from my lovely Crete holiday (minus) the attack, minding my own business while shopping in Iceland food store (not) the country Iceland! I get to the checkout, while I am in the queue this man out of nowhere starts a conversation with me. Here is what I recall from it:

ED: *"You have beautiful feet!"*

I looked around and saw this coolie (Indian) looking, mature man looking at me.

ME: *"Oh, thank you."*

What a lovely compliment to hear even more so from a stranger! As I was about to bend down to pick up my basket, he quickly whisked it up and started unpacking my items onto the counter (a true gentleman), I thanked him again and then said:

ME: *"Your lady is fortunate to have a gentleman like you."*

ED: *"I am still searching for her."*

ME: *"Oh... Ok!"*

ED: *"Would you mind if I take you out for dinner."*

I thought for a second and then said to myself, fu*k it, why not when I am 'single and free to mingle'. We introduced each other and exchanged numbers. When I got home, I decided to send him a short but sweet message, just letting him know it was a pleasure meeting him. About an hour later he rang to see what I was doing as he had a spare few hours before he had to get back to work. He asked if I wanted to meet for a drink and chat. I agreed and at the exact time we had decided he would pick me up; there he was knocking at my door; it was refreshing that he kept his word and was on time.

Then as we walked round to the front to what I thought was going to be a car was instead this beautiful Bentley limo was waiting for me to enter. Ed's a chauffeur driver of stunning vehicles and driving a variety of top clients and the public. As he went to open the door to let me in, I felt like a princess going to a ball, because that was how special he made me feel. There laid out on the side was a bottle of champagne and one glass. He poured me a drink of the champagne then sat back and just stared at me as I enjoyed the drink. It was me who started the conversation in the limo.

ME: *"I am surprised that a lovely gentleman like yourself is roaming around free and single or is it that you're so busy with work you don't have the time for anything else!"*

ED: *"No, no, no… it is not that. Anikka, I am going, to be honest with you from the bottom of my heart. I was in a relationship; she was from Port Orica. I was doing my job, as you call it. Listen, a relationship is built of trust."*

ME: *"Yes, of course."*

ED: *"It is based on honesty and loyalty."*

ME: *"Of course and respect all those for things."*

ED: *"Yep and I had gone to Paris for a week… I took a multi-millionaire guy who owns a school in Paris, and he wanted a car to hire for a week. I came back early; she did not expect me back that night and I came home and found her in my bed with a man."*

ME: *"I am so sorry. That is perhaps one of the worst things that anyone can experience in a relationship. Someone having an affair is one thing but to do it in the same bed, takes the ultimate piss!"*

ED: *"No, it is gone beyond another level because that is more than abuse that's mental torture. And I never stayed in that house again. I moved out and stayed away for eight months. That very night I packed my bags and moved out into a hotel and I said to myself I am going to put that house up for sale and the next day, that is what I did"!*

As we spoke more, I soon realised that the damage this woman had caused had now left him with severe trust issues and emotionally damaged which I could see in his eyes, he so wanted to be loved and seemed like he had lots of love to give as well. Here he is pouring out his heart to me while not even knowing me a full twenty-four hours talking about what sounded like a stunning, big eight-bedroom house up in Hamel Hempstead. But you know what the biggest joke of all was the fact that the girl had seven other rooms she could have used instead of the bed she shared with Ed, without a care in the world. What a selfish, bad-minded woman she was, its these types of females that give us decent, respectful ones a bad name! #KMT

We ended up going out to eat in a Chinese restaurant the next day in Queensway. Once again, Ed offered to collect me. I came out the front door and he was waiting to greet me with a big, warm hug and then we headed around the front of the house. Can you guess what car he had parked outside this time! A sexy big, white, and silver Rolls Royce, wow, what a car! There was me getting ready to open the door to get in, but before I could, Ed had beaten me to it and opened the door awaiting me to sit down so that he could close it behind me. Yep, I know what you're thinking, that is what he does anyway opening and closing the door for clients, but in my eyes, only real old skool gentleman like Ed takes pride in making a lady feel special (even when he is not working) but most of all, he loves his job! Providing a service where you drive people around is not an easy one as the truth be known probably 60% of clients are rude so you must have a certain tolerance level to provide this service.

I looked on the company's website to see what the client's reviews had to say about Ed and as expected; it was all excellent feedback. By day two, I could not believe my ears as it was most definitely a first-time experience to have someone declare that they had fallen in love with me, which is what Ed did. It was a Sunday afternoon on May 17th '2015 when I received a call from him while chilling at home. He had called to see how I was and to tell me about his day. The phone rings and I knew it was him before I even looked at the phone, having assigned the ringtone **"Always and Forever"** by the group Heatwave to his name, as that was the way he had made me feel. But I must say that a part of me was wishing it were Ali who was calling me. I was going through mixed emotions still thinking about him while having this new man Ed saying so many things and making me feel special in the space of two days of knowing him. Our conversation when I answered the phone.

ME: *"Hey"*

ED: *"Ms Forbes?"*

ME: *"Hello, Sir."*

ED: *"If this gets too much, tell me. I am sorry to ask you this, but I am going to ask you this question."*

ME: *"Sorry is not required; go ahead."*

ED: *"Have you ever thought about going into any business?"*

ME: *"I have always got ideas, but that's about it!"*

ED: *"It is ok, we'll talk when we're sitting and having dinner. I am just giving you an insight if you want to do something. Anything that is stopping you or whatever, we can talk about it and we can do things* together instead of you working for someone else you can work for yourself."

ME: *"Ok, that is something to think about. I have many things I want to do."*

ED: *"That's ok; we'll talk more when we get time."*

ME: *"Ok, thank you."*

Well, I certainly did not expect that, but there is a <u>first time for everything</u> having someone offer to help and invest in me starting my own business.

It was just so random, out of the blue and a lovely gesture! But my overthinking, wondering self could not understand why he had not done the same for himself, meaning started his own business. Instead of working for someone else it did not make sense, but on the other hand, it did, because Ed loves his job, he is a people's person and maybe he could not see himself doing anything else. So, investing in someone was his preferred choice!

Two weeks is how long this new possible romance lasted. Ed was never going to get around me being an Independent lady who was currently out of work while looking for new contracted work. Plus, like anyone still had bills to pay like my rent which was £1150.00 per month. He could not understand how I was supporting myself (err) little savings, which I tried not to touch, but I had no other means, so had to use my savings which thank god, got me through that high and low chapter of my life.

For this two-week relationship, it felt like a scene out of the movie **'Pretty Woman'** except I had none of the lavish hotels and gifts like Julia Roberts and Ed was not Richard Gere, but he was a lovely gent. Ed later confessed to me after the fourth/fifth day that he thinks I am a stripper or escort; part of me had a feeling that maybe he was thinking along those lines.

So, when I heard the words come out of his mouth, I was not surprised! Instead, I just started laughing then I felt myself get a little annoyed at the simple fact of him thinking I was lying about being out of work from contracting within construction. I thought he understood that I am a 'say how it is', straight-talking person!

Though I may have been successful, had that been the case as the way I see it (if that's your thing) might as well get paid for it, instead of giving it away for free! I may have been living the high life, with my own home (so no need to rent), no debts or struggles. Yes, I can admit back in my twenties I did contemplate trying out the 'Escort' industry just for companionship and dating, nothing sexual during the days when times were tough whenever out of work, or had little to no money for rent, food or to even get to interviews at times; it was only ever a thought never put into action.

I had even done some research into acting within the Pornography Industry, it is for a particular type of person this kind of work, in my opinion! I was curious to read about it but nothing more whereas the fetish industry is a piece of cake! There are lots of different fetishes, from basic 'foot worshipping' to more extreme like 'pleasure and pain' depending on the service required. It is like a 'pick and mix' where the service provider takes the lead, and some do not require physical contact. Have I had any fetish modelling experience, yes only once in my early twenties where a photographer needed a female for his client who requested 'face smothering'? Which is when a female sits on the man's face (underwear on) and smothers him. It was an easy peasy £200, I made that day!

There is lots of money to be made, again if this is your kind of thing and you can find genuine (non-creepy) clients. #EachToTheirOwn

I am not here to judge anyone, as I would be a hypocrite if I did because of what I am about to share with you. If I am honest, I did think about 'not' including it in this chapter BUT on the other hand why hide it as if I am (ashamed) of the experience when it was my choice, it defeats being an 'open book'. It was late '2011 when this took place, so it is relevant, which is why I am content to share it! A one-off experience which you may view as escorting; I beg-to-differ but were all entitled to our own opinion! Is it a big deal? I do not think so as it is a natural thing (sex), but this experience had an added unexpected bonus. #NoRegrets

I have had a 'one-night stand' no biggie (for some) as many people have these all the time, but I can confirm I have never had a one-night stand until the age of thirty, a first and last experience with a twist. I named it a **Paid One-Night Stand!** I once worked for a few weeks back in October '2011 in a Gentleman's Club, where ladies are paid a minimum of £50 per table for any table she hosts and socialises on which could vary from a one to one or a group of men, which would determine how many females would join the table. So even if you only got to sit at one table per night you were guaranteed to get some money in your pocket though £50 may not seem like a lot, trust me it is better than nothing! Sometimes a person will do almost anything if hungry or worried about the possibility of becoming homeless due to the rent not being paid. #LadyOfVariety

This club is a well-respected, clean, vibrant, and discreet place for all businessmen to chill, relax during the evening or early hours of the morning knowing they would be in great company with a variety of lovely females from all ethnicities ready and waiting to meet, greet and socialize with them.

Me being a novice to hosting in a Gentleman's Club, I can tell you it was a fun and eye-opening experience with music, so we could dance and keep ourselves entertained when it was quiet along with a few free drinks too. All the females were 100% in control in the club with a variety of options explained to me by the M.I.C. (man in control) alias name I have given the owner of the club. Staff were paid weekly, £50 to host at tables or £300 if you wanted to venture out and about outside the club at your discretion to a restaurant, club etc. or go straight to a room in the hotel above where both consenting adults could go and do as they pleased.

There was one black girl who had been working there for years; she had a young son of two and a partner who was at home with their child. My curious self-asked if her partner knew where she was working, she told me he knows she works in a club but not about the added extras! A few ladies had their regulars who would come to see and mingle with them, other mums whose partners or families were none-the-wiser, you had sisters, friends, and curious ones like (me) who was out of work, bored being at home alone with the same routine. I was living in a new area and wanted to try something different, meet new people and make some money.

Once just after midnight, me and two others were asked to join a table and host three guys who had been to a meeting, then out on the town but were not ready to go home. Bottles of champagne were flowing, while we were all talking, flirting, and having a laugh. Anyway, the guys wanted to get a room and invited us to join them, so we all agreed and made our way up to the hotel room. I popped to the toilet to have a ***"what am I doing"*** moment in the mirror; until when I finally emerged from the bathroom all I can say is, it was full steam ahead like a mini orgy going on! There they all were busy, kissing, licking, sucking, and fucking each other yet still had time to ask me to

"Come and join in"

Straight away (I told myself) sorry, not for me, mate! I am a one-on-one person only who is also very particular and can be scornful, i.e., hygiene and cleanliness. When I saw the three guys and two girls all over each other, it was far from a turn-on, but a big turn off! I did not join in or stay to watch; instead, I collected my things, opened the door, and left knowing I was still going to be paid £50 for sitting at the table plus the standard £300 for going outside the club. The next evening the two girls asked me why I had left, and I explained to them that it was not my kind of thing, so decided to leave them to it and go home! But there was this one occasion a couple of weeks later when this handsome, well-groomed businessman, who I had not seen before entered the club. I knew I had caught his eye from the moment he walked in as our eyes locked so when the boss informed me that the gentleman would like me to join him at his table.

I was pleasantly surprised and without a doubt attracted to him. We had a bottle of champagne as we sat talking and getting to know one another, he was an Accountant working in the city, I would say he was in his early to mid-forties and had a lovely personality to go with his good looks.

He had heard about the club from a friend so thought he would come to check it out and see what female companionship the club had; he certainly was at the right place.

After about an hour or two, he asked if I was hungry and wanted to join him for something to eat, of course, I agreed as I love my food'age. Lol! To cut a long story short YES, I did get **'Up, Close and Personal'** with him, which I enjoyed, even more as it had been a while since I had any action. He also held me close in his arms as we slept, which was lovely.

The following morning, he told me how much he had enjoyed my company and as we were leaving the hotel, he asked me to wait a moment as he quickly popped to the cash machine. When he returned, he opened my hand and placed some money in it and closed it back, I thanked him then he thanked me along with a kiss on my cheek and we went our separate ways. When I got back home and checked how much he had given me. I was pleasantly surprised, impressed, and grateful to have counted £300!

This extra £300 was not part of the service as all payments are directly from (the boss) owner of the club to the hostesses, so having him hand me the cash and thank me for my company, all I could think was OMG what an experience! £50 for hosting at the table, £300 for going out and an extra £300 so a total of £650 from my unexpected night, which is why I named this experience a **Paid One Night Stand**. The money that I made was enough for me to pay for the Voice-Over and Presenting courses I wanted to do, which I paid for the next day. I have been there, done that made some money and have no regrets. #DontJudgeMe

Concerning oral sex, I have never been a female that puts my mouth on any mans 'tings' aka penis. I can count on the one hand those who I have had a little play with but nothing to the extent of what men love from females and what majority females enjoy doing to men! The same way if a man is not into eating the (poom poom) aka vagina. I would not be upset with him because we all have personal choice, but his cock needs to be on point to compensate the penetration being as he does not want to give tongue stimulation to the clit. I know my 'middle section' is on-point, so regardless of me, not giving oral, my girl is more than enough, and never had any complaints! I briefly dated someone in the time that I worked at the Gentleman's Club; he had been a regular for years and it was only companionship and nothing physical between us. He was the owners' top customer who would call ahead before arriving at the club so that his drinks would be ready and waiting.

Two or four ladies would sit and conversate with him and sometimes he would even order in some pizza for us all to eat and enjoy while we sat at the table with him drinking champagne. A top-class man with a big heart, kind, thoughtful, caring, and generous, but there were two vital things that I grew concerned about in the time that I was working at the club. Even during our brief time dating, which was after I stopped working at the club due to finding new contracted work. SK, a charming mid-fifties, Caucasian, well-known man within his field of work and more. He was always shown nothing but love whenever we went out in particular at the bar of one of his favourite places, The Chesterfield Hotel in Mayfair.

We even stayed over in the hotel, shared a room and bed while cuddling throughout the whole night, it was not about sex but two people not rushing anything while continuing to get to know one another and enjoying each other's company. #NothingWrongWithThat

I will forever be thankful to him for being there for me when my Nan died. A sincere, genuine, big-hearted, straight-talking, no-nonsense man who enjoyed my company as did I his too. He made me feel special, was so easy to talk to and always wanted to know about me and my life growing up. He loved to spoil me too, having brought me three gifts on separate occasions.

They were classy and elegant presents; the first was a chain for my 31st birthday and then a bracelet a few weeks later when he took me shopping, both from the Tiffany and Co store. Plus, a stunning geometric knitted designer dress from Missoni the most expensive clothing or anything in fact, that I own! Would you believe the dress is still wrapped-up lovely in the bag, unworn all these years later due to not going out anywhere worthy of me wearing it! He always complimented me and a massive fan of my long legs; he loved it when I had them on show.

Who said real gents (do not exist) or that two people of the opposite sex can't enjoy being with one another without being intimate, well I am living proof that this is possible and 'SK' was all that and more? I was growing very fond of him, we spoke about him wanting more children, me wanting and maybe having them together. He is a doting father of one! A daughter (late teens/early twenties) but I could not help thinking that she may not approve of my age or being a **Lady of Colour**. We never met, but he had mention introducing me to his parents once, but I think my uncertainty of what they might think of me and getting upset at times for thinking that he did not really care for me but wanted to keep me a secret as to why we always went to the same places. Where was the logic in my thought; if your trying to keep someone a secret would you take them out to public places? No, so why was I thinking like this!

My insecurities were allowing negativity to take over rather than enjoying and appreciating the good times and positivity's. As 'SK' is a man who works hard, plays hard, enjoys having fun, socialising, helping others and all about positivity. The 'damaged goods' girl in me was partly to blame along with my concern about his health even more so having had him call me to inform me he was in hospital but would not allow me to visit him which upset me so much I broke down crying after I came off the phone to him. I could not understand why he would call to tell me he was in hospital but would not allow me to be by his side! This was the icing on the cake that I could not handle as rejection was all I was feeling, so removed myself completely but still checked in on him via text and email to make sure he was alright as I will always care.

For any female whose had that experience of working in a Gentleman's Club or as an Escort should not feel guilty or ashamed about this, because if they carry themselves in the right way and maintain self-respect then who is anyone to judge. I am sure there are many reasons why this type of work is available because everyone's circumstances are different and some females have a high sex drive, so this work is perfect for them. They can have unlimited sex, be in control of what sexual acts they do or do not do and get paid as **Time Is Money'** regardless of the field of work you are doing. #YerISaidIt

I have never declared to be Ms Goodie-Two-Shoes. Do I think less of myself for having a paid one-nightstand, not at all because it is an experience that is part of my life journey! Had I not been out of work, I would probably never have come across the 'hostess' ad or even worked there, but I did! Why, because it was already part of my path when God created me, simple!

Everything we go through in our individual life was already written, good or bad and just need to accept it! I can count on one hand (if that) those in my life that I can call genuine, real friends. For those that I have either removed myself from or the frenemies who pretend to be interested and happy for you by 'skinning teet' (smiling) in your face but yet you can feel their negativity and envy like a bad smell!

The same ones who love bitching to you about their other friends, so no doubt doing the same by chatting about you too, rather than being truthful by expressing how they feel about that particular friend or their scenario. I am sure they will have plenty to say about this experience should they read this book or hear about it, but hey as the saying goes.

> *"If people are not talking about you, then you're not doing something right."*

They have issues with you but instead of saying how it is they carry on and pretend like all is well, but you know better! It is best to leave them behind and out of your life. Evil aura is like an illness which can break you if you are unaware of it; so, the moment that you can see or feel it, you must be strong enough to let it go and remove yourself. Who has got time for these so-called friends or family, not me! I am too grown, honest and real to entertain anyone's fake'arage, which is why I feel no way to remove myself from friends, family, or foe as sometimes you have to do that to grow or protect yourself. I have spoken about writing a book for too long and this first book is the one of possibly three like a **'Trilogy'** reflecting on the most memorable and significant moments in my life from 2011 to 2016/18.

I still have another 'ten years' worth of diary material from 2010-2000 to share with you, the reader, though not much written between 2000-2002!

But let us move on and let me share a little more about some of the men who passed through my life in the last six years. There was a brief encounter with someone for a few weeks back in July '2011 who I referred to as Mr Parker, who I met through Drama School in our early thirties. A black man with two kids and a complicated relationship. Once when going out to eat, he asked me not to wear any <u>underwear</u>, having seen my article in 'The Sun Newspaper' about me enjoying going 'commando' at times, which was a turn-on for him! It was our first evening spent together. A night that neither of us will ever forget as it was Saturday 23rd July the day that the fantastic, beautiful, and talented Amy Winehouse (R.I.P) had died.

We could not believe it and spent the rest of the night playing all her tunes and had only got 'up, close and personal' a handful of times which was all good; but all I will say is he was in my life one minute then gone the next! We kept in contact by writing and the odd phone call.

Then in '2012, I was seeing a friend of a friend (cast member) from a Theatre Production that we were doing together. He introduced us; we clicked straight away with instant attraction! A Jamaican born, mid-late thirties man with Locs from Birmingham, a middle-weight boxer who I had named 'Bad Boy' and was a real lady's man, with a few kids and a great father to them all. I loved getting away up to his as I was always made to feel right at home, not to mention he was a superb cook and great sex every time. We were seeing each other as and when for a couple of years and though I liked him I did not allow myself to get close to him emotionally as he knew I was not too keen on how many baby mothers he had; all I knew is I was not going to be one! Though he is a great father, and it was nothing personal, merely an **'I don't want'** as I had always been adamant about not getting seriously involved with a man who had children with more than one or two (max) women. So, my mindset was simply good times, great sex, and nothing more.

Back in '2013 on the way home from work walking through Hammersmith Mall I met a guy who saw me walking past and approached to introduce himself. Then he started explaining to me about the charity he was raising money for and asked me to sign up. I nick-named him 'Charmer' simply because he was very charming as mentioned in **Chapter 6** and was seeing him on and off for a year. I later found out he had a girlfriend, due to there being a few female items around his flat, when I asked him about it, he tried to say it was his ex-partners' things then later confessed that they were 'on and off'. Joker! So, I refused any more action only oral pleasure!

I did not appreciate seeing him (once) snorting 'cocaine' in front of me, had he asked if I minded, then I would have told him not to do it around me, which I did anyway and that was the first and last time he took it while I was present.

What drugs a person uses is up to them; though I will never understand how people can put anything up their nose! Nor would I want to be around anyone who was 'injecting'. It was after taking the 'white stuff' that he found extra confidence to reveal himself to me like that; I always knew what he was going to do whenever he popped out of the room. To one point I had enough of seeing him on a 'high' and was not impressed, so decided to lock-off all contact and stayed away, ending that chapter!

Over the years, I have either had fun, dated, or been involved with men from all background's successful, x2 known UK Actors/Comedian, Bad boys who have done the crime then the time at HMP, a Photographer, Property owners to name a few including internet Dating Sites. I am an open-minded person so whether it be a fu*k buddy, to dating (wining or dining) or non-exclusive relationship, they have all been respectful! A few guys admitted that they have found me a little intimidating, hard to read or unapproachable, but it did not keep them away; otherwise, I would not have these experiences to share!

I even had an office **'Naughty but Nice'** encounter with my Site Manager while I was working on a project which was great fun. The chemistry had been there for months and he even confessed that he wanted to 'bend me over' which was a 'turn on' as we both knew it was a matter of time that we would get it on! A few of our text conversations exchanged leading up to our first encounter.

HIM: *"That's a sexy outfit your wearing"*

ME: *"Thank you, you're looking rather scrumptious yourself."*

HIM: *"You need to start wearing bin bags to work and I won't get the urge to taste you!"*

ME: *"Lol, cheeky... stop it your making me blush. You naughty boy"*

HIM: *"What colour panties are you wearing?"*

ME: *"Will give you a sneak preview"*

HIM: *"Can't we go somewhere in the building. I need to taste you"*

ME: *"Looking for somewhere so u can 👅 ((tongue) emoji"*

The only location I could find was the female toilets which are not an ideal place, but they were nice, clean, and roomy. The sex was great, a dangerous high at getting caught and we met at least once most days and even managed to have sex in the office where we worked right on top of the desk! Our office naughtiness lasted just over two months before I moved on to pastures new, having also had one home visit 'servicing' from him too. It was most def fun and exciting while it lasted with Mr Professor the alias name, I referred to him by at times. You know who you are! #ImNoAngel #YouOnlyLiveOnce

The magnificent true story of Tina Turner's life in the film starring American actor Angela Bassett called; **What's Love Got to Do with It** who plays Tina Turner and Laurence Fishburne as Ike Turner, her abusive former husband. In the film, Tina fell hard and fast for the older and handsome Ike. But from the start, Ike showed her little to no respect but exploited her talents to help gain notoriety for his music career. After years of infidelity, drug abuse, sexual assault and physical abuse, Tina finally began to love herself enough to leave him. It took the intervention of her friend and former backup singer to help her see that she did not deserve what Ike was doing to her as she was a strong, beautiful woman whose husband was intimidated by her and the growing success her career was having so the only way for him to take charge and remain in control was to abuse her physically and mentally. In the end, Tina realised that her feelings of love for Ike were not enough to keep her in an unhealthy, abusive relationship even more so for the sake of her children!

I am sure many women can relate to some of the emotions Tina was wrestling with before leaving Ike. Thankfully, I have never been with anyone like this and if I am honest, I think I would end up causing either serious damage or death (worst case scenario) to any man who tried to raise his hand/fist to me, if my Dad did not get to him first! That is one thing I would NEVER accept. Protecting myself is the priority unless I were a mother, then my child/ren would come first. I would do a prison sentence instead of enduring years of abuse full of nothing but bruises, fear, hurt and pain. I am a loyal person, but I am not one who would stay with someone who shows me no respect and honour. I would rather be single than stuck in a miserable relationship because.

"I can do bad all by myself"

Real love is supposed to be beautiful, not painful! Regardless of your gender if you are in a relationship where the words

"I am sorry, I won't do it again"

Has been heard more than twice (second chances), then that is an unhealthy abusive relationship, and you need to get out! Having witnessed my mums' treatment for years from the father to her (youngest two) was enough to educate me about what is right (honour and love) and what is wrong (abuse and control) only one will I accept! Every female has a princess locked inside of her, wanting to meet her prince; but often, we look for a spouse or lover to complete us then end up disappointed when it does not happen.

Love for someone should not determine your value or self-worth!

There comes a time as you grow inside with confidence and self-love; you will attract someone who is at the same place in their life as well. If a man is not mature enough as I am sure some females would agree that no amount of wining and dining, flowers, chocolates, or gifts can compensate, therefore he would not stand a chance with me. Many men think females are difficult to understand, but really, we are not! We express and walk in the fullness of our humanity, were meant to be admired, adored, and pleasing to the eye it is our **Prerogative** whereas men are conditioned to be more guarded and hostile.

If all men treated and respected females in the same way, they would expect another man to treat their mum, sister, or daughter I believe there would be more fruitful, long-lasting, and loving relationships in the world today!

Coming into the knowledge of who I am as a Nigerian (mixed like seasoning) descendant lady and more specifically one who has recently heard of my royal bloodline has not made it any easier or brought me closer to finding my partner. African women as all women deserve love, honour, respect, honesty, and loyalty from their lovers. The African woman has always valued the power of family and community living and she knows that a healthy nation must start with a strong family and for her, that family starts with her man. These relationships have been uplifting, empowering, loving, oppressive and lonely all at the same time. Truth be told life is filled with contradictions when it comes to any relationship in general, but that is the beauty of understanding one another and compromising as and when needed!

The African woman was held in high regard by the African man. In her, he knew that his seed would continue upon the earth through his lineage. Even today, in traditional African spirituality, the woman is represented through their understanding of God. African men understood that it was through the woman that a keener understanding of the lord would be seen.

The Akan/Ashanti people of Ghana understand the male and female aspect of God. The Akposso of Togo believe that when God made humans, he had to make the woman first so that she would be the carrier of the seed to populate the earth and that seed came from God. African men honoured their women very highly at one time; their instinct knew there needed to be a balance between the genders. He drew from her wisdom and strength; she was his source of life. And if you think about it, this principle is fully accurate. When a child is within the womb of the woman for nine months, the baby is solely dependent on the mother for nutrients, protection, and space to develop.

The miracle of motherhood is something only God could have created and wonder to behold. The miracle of a wise woman's influence helps to build families, tribes, and nations and at one time the African woman was the envy of the world, but the impact of outsiders changed all of that. Learning about these things is not only essential but also helpful to me as I continue to grow into a lady, not yet a woman until I carry life in my stomach and become a Mum by God's grace. #Amen

The hope of the African culture is the African male and female coming together as equal co-creators and not one dominating over the other but with distinctive roles and responsibilities. Most African women today, whether living on the continent of Africa or in the diaspora, do not want to sit at home and tend the house. It is not that she does not love her family because she does but wants to make sure she gives them all the absolute best of herself. She knows there is more to her than being at home and has a built-in need to release and show it. Coming into the knowledge of my royal bloodline has empowered me. It makes me feel so proud of my Great-Granddad, but most of all, my precious, loving, and beautiful Grandma **Princess Elizabeth Adebimpe Adepoju (nee Haastrup).** Even more so when my Dad tells me I have her energetic nature and personality.

I feel extra special being her first-born grandchild who she adored, loved, and was always so delighted to see me and I am fortunate to have known and still remember my Grandma, who I love and miss tremendously till this day. Yes, I have had my fair share of disappointments from men and maybe some were not worthy of me or my time, but still have no regrets to those who I had hoped to connect with on all three levels (physical, emotional, and spiritual) as these are important. I want a partner for a lifetime, not for a moment!

I am a patient lady and sometimes my ***"kindness is taken for weakness"*** by men and people in general, but that is a quality in me that will never change.

So, for me as well as all young girls, ladies, and women, we have all got to embrace ultimate self-love as a priority to ourselves; because if you do not love yourself first, then there is no way you will be able to love someone else. #selflove

It Is Better To Have Nobody,

Than to Have Someone

Who is Half There,

Or Does Not Want

To Be There"

Angelina Jolie

#SelfLove

CHAPTER 9: MAN, OVER CHILD

My mum was born in December 1956 and is of mixed-race ethnicity, her father was Jamaican, and her mother was half White and Jamaican. A mother of four, with three grandchildren in her early sixties who could pass for being in her forties. I have always been proud of whenever people complimented her youthful looks and personality. She has always been a fun, down to earth and beautiful person, regardless of my upbringing this fact will never change about her! She is the second eldest, her sister (Aunt Bev) was the firstborn, who was raised and still lives back in Jamaica. Then her three younger siblings, two sisters and a brother, were all born and raised here in London alongside her. I think my aunt Bev was left in Jamaica at the tender age of 3-6mths due to Nans' Dad being furious about her falling pregnant again so shipped her off to the UK without her child.

Unfortunately, Nans official firstborn, was a boy, who died!

The Forbes sisters back in the 70s/80s were all well-known growing up on the notorious North Peckham Estate in South-East London, they were known (in my eyes) for throwing the best house-parties. They were loved and admired by many, had a close sisterhood relationship and were all beautiful females. Many men adored them, and I am sure they had their fair share of haters too! For me, the early eighties up to the age of 3-5 were and still are my best memories of my mum, Dad, and aunts. Perhaps it was because I was so young and innocent, I love looking back on photos from back then, reliving those memories. I was nineteen when mum decided to move (again) from being a free, single mum who was independent and had just had her fourth child. My baby brother was the new addition to the family conceived in 1999 when her ex-boyfriend/stepdad (younger siblings Dad) took us on holiday to Tobago. Her relationship with him over the years was unhealthy and toxic.

But now she had a second child for him; and decided to give their relationship another try by moving into the new house that he had brought down the road. He was one of those men who had the 'short man syndrome'. A bully, who was controlling, mentally and physically abusive with no respect where my mum was concerned. The man did not deserve my mum or her love, nor did I appreciate him putting her down for having two children from two different men. Mum is one of the most beautiful, funny, witty, and young hearted people you could ever meet, who you are guaranteed to have good times with no matter where you are! When it came to him the (*short arse*) mum did not know her worth, she allowed him to humiliate her in public, in front of family and friends too.

Then the issues between my mum and me started when she allowed him to have the final say over 'any and everything' that concerned me! He did not let me go home after school (teenager) instead I had to go and look after my little sister at his mums, who I love and adore, and she treated me like one of her grandchildren. The simple fact was I could not shit without my mum telling me to always **"Go and ask D"** like WTF! Allowing a man who is not the father of your child to have the final say, is something **no mother should do,** trust me! I will never forget, and cannot as I witnessed too much, but I have forgiven mum for allowing this man to have control over my day-to-day life.

To me, it is the most shameful, wrong, and disturbing thing a parent can do. Men will come in and out of your life, but your children are your responsibility and yours forever, whether you like it or not! No partner should ever come between a parent and child. Unfortunately, mum always put him before me, so any female that does this in my eyes is a mother who I refer to as someone who puts her man before her child. #ManOverChild

Saturday, 1ˢᵗ October 2000, was when mum moved back in with him. They were going to start again as one family, without me, just a five-minute walk to Hazelbank Road from where my mum was previously living with three of her four children in Catford, SE6. It was a well-known address between 2000-2003 when I officially had my independence and was living on my own, having plenty of fun. I invited an old school friend to share with me and rent my spare room. Both of us were experiencing living without our parents, for the first time, doing as we pleased, when we wanted. It was the spot where everyone (friends and friends of friends) was always welcome and enjoyed coming around, day and night. Good times with a few parties, BBQs, with plenty dramas along with one or two unexpected situations too but most of all I can 100% agree with the saying.

"You don't know someone until you either live or go on holiday with them."

So, let us just say on a few occasions, my experience living with her was far from pleasant due to what I saw regarding her hygiene and cleanliness, which was not of the norm. Not for me, anyway! #EachToTheirOwn #NoRegrets

Truth be known, it was not by choice that I was made to live alone, but mum made the decision to try again for the third time with a man that was never worthy of her in the first place but always seemed to have something over her which made her go back to him. What made it even worse was the fact that mum had my two younger siblings in tow with her and once again, I no longer had any siblings living under the same roof as me. Yet just like my older brother (who I did not grow with either) as our Nan was his full-time guardian. I was and felt segregated from my two younger siblings who I adored to the moon and back and so wished mum did not move out, but she did!

It broke my heart as I longed for a baby sister for years, she was six when mum moved out in '2000. I was 'thirteen' years old when she was born in March '1994 and they named her Rhea.

Then by the time I was 'nineteen' the new addition (brother) arrived, and they named him Lewis, born, in March '2000. I could not get enough of them both as babies, the number of pics I took of them both, says it all! Hand on heart during the time when mum was pregnant with my baby brother, I was not happy; in fact, I was disgusted at the fact that his semen was growing inside of my mum again! To anyone who knows the lyrics from this heart wrenching, upsetting song called **Love Is Blind** by American rapper Eve. You can hear the pain when listening to this tune; it is deep! I can relate to how angry she felt seeing her friend being abused, though he was not as brutal to my mum. But I would have done the same thing by taking his life had he taken my mums to the grave. #RealTalk

How a mother can put their children second to any man is not only irresponsible but also selfish and embarrassing. I now know that my mum was an emotionally broken woman because of the abuse she suffered from her mother and she was looking for love and acceptance giving him the power to control and mentally/physically abuse her too. Lucky for him, he was never stupid enough to put his hands on me, because even he knew that would have been the last time, he ever used that hand again! Too many children are victims of abuse or sexual assault from their mothers' partners. The mum cares more about keeping their man satisfied instead of the safety and protection of their child/ren.

"Never Put Your Partner, Before Your Child"

As mentioned previously I was Thirteen when mum had my baby sister, her third child. Everyone, from my neighbours to friends, in and out of school knew how excited and happy I was to finally have a sister of my own, although I had my older brother. I think I was between the age of

(1-5) when my older brother stopped living with mum and me. My younger sibling's Dad was a man I grew to despise. I was twenty-three when I stopped speaking to him and thirteen-years later I have no regrets for the choice I made back then due to all he put my mum through with his disrespect, cold and unaffectionate ways all from a man I once referred to as a stepdad. He too is not worthy of being mentioned in this book but was present for many years during parts of my primary, secondary and early twenties. He is a prime example of the kind of man **NOT** to entertain in my life at any time because time is precious, and they are not worthy if for most of the time your unhappy.!

Still, he is the only man that I recall causing my mum so much heartache, tears, low self-esteem, physical, mental abuse, and sickness. As to this day, I blame him for my mum suffering from **Bell's Palsy** (a type of facial paralysis that results in an inability to control the facial muscles on the affected side). It can be brought on by stress! The symptoms can vary from mild to severe. It may include muscle twitching, weakness, or total loss of the ability to move one or rarely both sides of the face. Had I not noticed straight away that there was something wrong with mums' face and rushed her to hospital, who knows if she would have recovered from it! I witnessed first-hand his treatment towards her, and I have ZERO tolerance for any man like him or any that has similar traits, though we cannot help who we fall in love with, so easier said than done sometimes.

I remember back in 1993-1994 when we had left Peckham for the second time having both been temporarily staying with Nan until mum found us somewhere else to live. That somewhere was Catford, on George Lane to be precise in a 2 bed flat only a few minutes' walk to the high street where the big cat statue, sits! It was on two occasions within the (bedroom and living room) while in my bedroom I could hear him shouting/arguing with my mum as she was crying, so I ran in to see what was happening and there he was pinning mum by the neck down on the bed.

Then there was another time when mum moved us again up the road to the better side of Catford off Bromley Road, except this time there were three of us mum, me, and my baby sister. He had convinced mum to move in with him to his four-bedroom house on Aaron Road, the worst mistake Mum could have made plus one she did not learn from otherwise she would never have moved into his second house back in '2000, this time leaving me behind.

As always, her only concern was him, their two children, the home, and the pretence perfect family life which I understand (to a degree) as she loved him, and the heart wants what the heart wants even if the person is not worthy of you! There was a time when my older brother came to visit for the day. We were sat in the living room and could hear him arguing with my mum, for me it was nothing new but not for my brother. So, he decides to go and see what is happening and I follow, we see them both by the stairs then two-twos his grabbed then pinned mum up against the wall — trying to intimidate and rough her up. I started shouting and crying out of anger at him to let her go, which is when my brother got involved and went up the stairs to protect mum!

They both ended up fighting down the stairs. He always had the upper hand; it was his house, so he kicked my brother out and mum had (as the saying goes) <u>made her bed and was lying in it</u>, while her innocent children suffered the consequences. That was the day I vowed **never** to live under the same roof as this man again! Unfortunately, mum was 'love blind' when it came to him despite all his negativity, aggression, and insults. Therefore, she was not strong enough; otherwise, there would have been no third chance! But my firm belief that our **'destiny has already been mapped out'** by God so mums is no different and I accept it!

Therefore, all that she/we both experienced was meant to happen. I know some of you either will not agree or maybe not understand what I mean, but I believe **'none of us is in control of our destiny'** the same way we cannot control our <u>fate.</u> Two things none of us know is how long we have to live or how we die. #Fact

My ex-stepdad being a hardcore smoker added to him being paranoid and aggressive but for any man to raise his hand to a woman or visa-versa needs to be shown a good lesson, so they will never do it again! I do not care if that man is a family member, friend, associate, or foe; there is never an excuse to abuse a woman just because your fragile ego needs to feel in control and domineering. I think the same about women too who abuse men! Abusers are insecure and feed of hurting and bullying. Let me give a little background on my mum to help you get a better understanding of why she is who she is. A mother of four children aged 40, 36, 23 and 17 in the order of boy, girl, girl, and boy. My older brother and I are the eldest (different Dads, same mother) the two youngers have the same father.

My older brother and I always lacked love, time, affection and help from our mum which was something I accepted from a young age whereas my older brother, till this day still craves it all from her. I suppose this is due to living and being raised by our Nan. It sometimes-caused jealousy, envy and dislike between my brother and me, which also saw us fight many times worse than a cat and dog. Whenever Del and I were fighting, if he hurt me by putting me in a headlock, punching me etc. to the point where I was in tears. I knew there was only one thing that I could do to make him stop plus to hurt him back! So, I would open my mouth wide like a crocodile, latch my teeth anywhere I could get hold of him then bite him **hard** and he would stop! I know it was not a good thing to do, but I had to defend myself somehow and this was all I had in my defence.

Growing up, we were both made to feel like a burden, unwanted, disliked at times and as a result experienced overall emotional abandonment. Perhaps because mum was never given unconditional love by my Nan (her mum) which made her the way she is towards us or because we both had two different fathers. Neither of them did mum care to talk about nor did she fail to let us know that in her eyes they were 'no good'! A mother and fathers love, and support are vital in the healthy development of a child.

But because my mum never received it, she did not know how to give it to us growing up, so was parenting out of what she believed was correct because that is all she had to offer. I know from as young as I can remember her ways towards me were not (at times) of a loving, devoted mum and till this day she never likes talking about the past. Anything to do with either our Dads, why she left my brother in the care of my Nan; or putting that man before us are unspoken. Explaining or saying sorry is not what mum does when it comes to her older two children!

It is brushed under the carpet when I challenge her with questions from back then in the seventies and eighties. I believe she may still be a broken woman who will deny or even forgotten some of the things mentioned in this book, but it is **my view, my truth**, **my words** of **my life** during those years living with her and alone. I am thirty-six now and for the last six years, the stable relationship we had all those years (minus) any dramas or problems is no more. We met up once for a catch-up after three years and this is what I wrote in my diary on that day.

Saturday 19th September '2015: Been awake since 06:30 am, it is now 19:14and I am on the tube heading home having just spent the last 6hrs catching up with mum who I have not seen since my Nans funeral back in February '2012. I waited for her at the entrance/exit of the DLR and we greeted each other with a hug, as she hugged me, she broke down crying (did not expect that), but she calmed down within a few minutes which was good. Honestly, I thought I would have been the one that would have broken down crying but surprised myself, that I did not! Maybe because of all the tears I had shed over the years, as we started to talk, the first thing Mum said was

"I don't want to talk about the past."

Then I explained for (us) to move on it was something that had to be addressed in today's meeting so we could get it out in the open, otherwise what is the point! Mum did not want to hear the truth, but certain things had to be spoken about like my older brother and the Drama, her man over child ways and the Crete holiday where her granddaughter attacked me. Though I wanted to air the Nanny situation, I decided not too as I did not want to upset or hurt her as I am sure I would have broken down crying! I tried to keep it to a minimum though I did get a little annoyed, but think I done well, so I am proud of myself. Mum updated me about other family members, though I (did not) ask, as I explained to her that my priority is **our** relationship despite anyone else as they all decided to stop all contact with me and take sides, not realising it was the wrong move to make as I am not begging anyone to talk to me!

Mum and I have met up again and talking, so that is all that matters. But it is all good as I expressed all that I think was necessary and some of what I wanted to get off my chest though I could have conversed more. I was not trying to upset mum or anything like that, so that is it; a new chapter and we will take each day as it comes, and the rest is in god's hands. In the past, there were many times when I would start writing this book, but it always became too hard and emotional. Then I would begin guilt-tripping and condemning myself with thoughts that perhaps I should not expose. It is all true, I have no reason to lie and this is one part of my life that I am free to speak my truth of what I experienced, what I saw and remember when I was growing up!

I am telling my story, the good, the bad and the ugly. Everyone should take ownership of their own life story no matter how difficult it may be. We owe it to our higher selves to accept whatever happened in our life in order to move on. I know mum may never accept her mistakes, but if I had kept the resentment in my heart that I carried for so many years, I would not have moved on with my life by removing myself in-order-to grow. It still pains me to see the effects my mum's behaviour has on my older brother whom she never raised due to whatever the reason, though my Dad recently told me when I had asked him why my brother was with my Nan and this was his response.

"Because your Nan wanted to keep him, but at any point, your brother could have returned to live with your mum, but he preferred living in Peckham at your Nans because she spoiled him rotten and he was her favourite grandchild."

Would my brother agree, I do not know! I recall from the age of about six/seven we had left Peckham for the first time back in the mid-eighties having had my mum and aunt M (her youngest sister) buy a house together in Abbey Wood, SE2. I had the best of both worlds living with my favourite aunt who I admired and was my role-model but even more critical at times she was more like a mum to me during the time the three of us lived together.

Like most children, I would love sleeping in my mums' bed, cosied up next to her. It gave me a sense of warmth, peace, and comfort as it would any child. I would be either just falling asleep or watching tv in her bed till I fell asleep until the doorbell rang and then hear a voice – it was him, my mum's boyfriend aka ex-stepdad. Gosh, it was annoying when he just turned up all hours of the night as I knew what that meant for me, so would pretend I was deep in sleep hoping mum would not disturb me. Yerrrr, right!

Sometimes she would carry me or wake me to get up and go into my bed. Even if I moaned and cried, it did not stop me from leaving her warm bed to go into my cold bed and try to get back to sleep. I hated it and thought, why could she not leave me in her bed and stay downstairs instead! Why a mother believes that this is acceptable towards their child. All it had done was make me resent her ways while growing up due to my mixed emotions of feeling unwanted, unworthy, unloved, pushed out and alone. Not to mention having trust issues too! Yes, on the outside, I may look like a cold-faced bitch, without a care in the world. However, it does not change the fact that there are some issues I am still healing from today as I continue to grow every day, while trying to curb my mouth more, LMFAO!

I think of royal and straight away my only favourite person springs to mind, the late Princess Diana. She was stunningly beautiful, delightful, and charming. Unlike the other royals, Princess Diana was relatable to all whether they were commoners or royalty. But under the surface, it is said that she was suffering from anxiety, depression, and a sense of insecurity. Did her emotional issues stem from things that happened in her childhood, like mine? Was her marriage into the royal family the thing that broke her down?

Had she been a commoner, would she have suffered as much emotionally? So many questions we can only speculate the answers to because our beloved 'English Rose' Princess is no longer with us. She met her fateful end in Paris in '1997 through a fatal car accident. I am sure there is so much Princess Diana wanted to tell the world, but now we will never know!

For me writing this book is also helping me to release and heal from my past scars left inside of me, which I hope in time will mend completely. Although I am an open book, I have never been one to offload my childhood experiences because it is a sensitive and delicate subject. Sharing trauma from your past takes courage. I know that writing diaries for all these years have helped me to express what I could not speak out loud as many would never think that these things had happened. They look on the outside and maybe see a stern, cheeky, pleasant, lovely, bold, and confident lady but do not see my fears and insecurities. I have kept a lot bottled up inside over the years and believe this may be a contributor to my bouts of depression.

Who would think that a girl born and raised in London would be given a false surname upon birth by her parents to hide her identity? Or that my surname-name should be (but is not) either Adepoju or Forbes-

Adepoju on the birth certificate, to then find out years later about the historical Nigerian Royal Bloodline and would be horribly, abused by her Nan? You could not make this stuff up!!! It is all part of my life and I have accepted it and hope to become the inspirational lady/woman, that I am destined to be! I am sure; if you think about your own life, there are stories that many would not believe had happened to you. But that is the thing about life and knowing or understanding people; each one of us has a story and carries a purpose.

And we should not run away from any of it. I believe a great contributor to depression is the section of the past within our brain that we have not dealt with, healed from therefore unable to move forward. We instead try and fool ourselves by either ignoring, blocking or 'depress it' into our subconscious mind, tucked away and hiding. But the outward signs of depression are indicators that there is something under the surface that we are hurting from and it has us locked away from experiencing the full essence of our lives and best versions of ourselves. I am a realist whose direct, outspoken, honest and I am sure too stubborn at times also, I know that my child, teenage and adult life is nothing compared to others who have experienced far worse.

Despite anyone's view, after reading this book, I had accepted my past many years ago, what happened has happened! I can only hope that I find happiness, love, and stability through the remainder of my life journey here on out, taking one day at a time, by gods' grace. #Amen

As a child, you are in a very vulnerable state. I did not have the means to walk out and leave my mum behind, but thankfully I had my Aunty M's house to escape to whenever things got too much at home. It took for her to choose him over me, her second child to finally accept that I am pretty much on my own in this world, so I either learn how to make the best of it or perish in self-pity. I certainly have not got time for that!

Now I realise that although my parents pretty much neglected me because though I lived with my mum, she was not the same with me after she split with my Dad. Dad was a ninety-per cent absent Dad (regardless of how much he says he tried to see me) the fact is he missed too many vital years of my life and will never know how much I cried, longing for him to come and take me away at times, but it never happened! I am an adult no longer a child who can give myself as much attention, love and self-care needed to become stronger. Writing is a dose of medicine for me! It ignites the creative process of life within me every time I do it. Letting me express everything with no boundaries precisely the way I speak, which is not perfect, but it is genuine!

It is an honest, humorous, and hopefully, inspiring non-fiction book and thank you again for reading it. For anyone reading this who may have gone through similar or worse; **"Believe in Yourself"** and try to find a way to offload so you can express yourself, to let go of the past. Most of my life experiences have been via another person. I had devoted my life around them; their happiness always came before mine. I was their rock, friend, daughter, and supporter in their times of need and this person is my mum! I feel at my age now (thirty-six) I have had my fair share, gone through many testing times and had my youth sacrificed due to having to grow up too quickly.

Through all of this, I never got to experience unconditional love which is what every parent owes their child. I believe in the 'Law Of Attraction' so what we spend most our time thinking and speaking about is the reality we will create for our lives which is why we should all try to think more positively, though easier said than done! #NoteToSelf

Everything happens for a reason; it is not for me to understand why my journey had to endure what it did! At times it may have broken me (to a degree) suffering in silence with depression, I did not allow it to have a complete hold over me. I have continued to fight back with my thoughts, one-million-per cent stronger, plus a more determined lady who knows how hard to read and cold I can come across sometimes!

Regardless of anything, I know my heart is pure plus I am a good person. #SelfLove #RealTalk

Although my mother may have chosen **man over child** as her life's mantra that is not ever going to be my choice. You can only hope and try to be the best, loving and caring parent for your child as there are no instructions on how to be a parent, so you learn as you go along. For me being around or looking after children of all ages since the age of 8/9 has always been second nature, from looking after family and friends' kids to my cousins, godchildren, and siblings and yes, I can say I am strict but fair! I can only hope that should I ever be blessed to become a mother my child/ren will mellow me and emboldening my inner child so that I may finally get healed by providing my own child (one day) with love, quality time, affection and making sure they know they come first!

Neither Nan nor mum dealt with their childhood pain, hurt, tears or unanswered questions; therefore, their dysfunction was passed down from mother to daughter and as a result, I suffered. I know my mum's life was not an easy one. During her childhood, she was emotionally mistreated by her mother, had two children by two different men by the age of twenty-four, plus the abortions before/after I was born. To this day, when I think about the extra siblings that I could have had, it breaks my heart which is why I do not believe in terminations because every life is a blessing! It has given me an even keener outlook on the value of innocent life that comes from God. But I am not my mum, so I do not know what she may have been thinking or going through back then as to why she made those choices to end life!

Females have reasons why they do what they do, and it is not my place to judge anyone who has done this, but I am entitled to my own opinion on this topic, as are you! I know that if mum had not chosen this option, I would have had other siblings all from the same father and maybe a better relationship with them unlike my non-existent relationship from the last seven years with my younger two siblings! If Rhea and Lewis cared about me or our relationship, they would have kept in contact and wanted to meet up etc.

But neither of them did, none of them was babies back in '2011, she was 17and he was 11years old. The same way neither of them can ever say I told them not to contact me or that I did not want to stay in their life, but the truth is we did not grow together so me being out of the picture was no biggie. I never had that close connection with any of them as I would have liked growing up, more so with my sister, it was always a struggle; trying with someone who did not really want to know!

Maybe she felt the same resentment towards me the same way I did towards my older brother Del, when I was younger when he would come around to spend time with mum. I felt like he was taking my mum away from me which is why I rarely liked him coming around or staying over. So, I get it! That is how she or both of them may have felt towards me because that is a feeling a child experiences when sharing their parent with an outsider (me). Because I was not living with them!

I remember on **Tuesday 6th Sep '2016** via FB I had seen a message from her, which had been sent to me four years prior (24.07.2012) but had only just seen it, why I do not know! The message reads.

RHEA: *Hey, Nik!! Missing you loads, how are you? Xxxxxx*

I responded (four yrs. later) better late than never having only just seen it!

ME: *Hi Re, not sure why I have only just seen this message from you while clearing out my inbox apologies 4yrs later. Hope ur well.x*

As expected, she did not respond! But my first thought when I had seen the message was **"Err, why message me on FB"** when she could have called me had she really wanted to know how I was doing, but she did not! Even receiving this type of message from her was a little strange as she has never been that younger sister from the age six upwards who made much of an effort. Both her and my younger brother have not been a part of my life since '2011 and probably never will be again, but will always be here for them, and wish them both the best. I will always love and miss them and hope they know how lucky and fortunate they are for growing, bonding together plus having the same father, unlike their two older siblings!

Here is the last diary entry dated **Tuesday 8th Nov '2011** from mum upset and complaining to me (like always) but this time it was about Rhea, Titled.

INTERVIEW 4 JSA @JOBCENTRE | 1ST TIME CRISIS LOAN | MUM IN TEARS

Dear Diary, I was feeling so hungry @00: 15am, that I went and had the only microwaveable food that I could eat which was Beans and Cheese and it went down like a treat. I got up after 12pm again today, though I was not really sleeping more thinking and did not rush to get up because I did not have to be at the Job Centre till 2pm. I went for my appointment and have my first sign-on date on the 17th and looked at a leaflet about getting a 'crisis loan' and contacted the number.

They asked 10 questions and they were able to give me £88.01 which I was grateful for and had to go to 'Acton' Job Centre to get the payment, then cash it at the post office. I went and put the gas back on (a wk. later) £30, then £5 went on debt and on the electric, which was on
emergency and had £19.95 left on it, amen.

I had spent £40 on food and when I got home, I made 'chicken tikka masala' and had x2 smoked salmon with Philadelphia cheese while I waited for the food to cook. Then at about 7pm, I had a call from mum sounding upset and then started crying, then she told me Rhea had left home yesterday after being horrible to Lewis about him possibly having piles. Mum told her off and she packed and left! Then mum started saying we all have no respect for her.

Then I started to tell her some home truths about herself saying, 'at least Rhea never had to take on independence by herself at 19' due to not wanting to live back under the same roof as my ex-stepdad.

But as always Mum can never accept that she put 'Man Over Child' when it came to him and me. I remembered I had an interview appointment at 7pm for a 'control worker' in the cab office down the road, so went to that and have to return tomorrow at 12pm for training and while I was walking back, I sent Mum a text saying.

"Just to say regardless of what you think of me, you are my mum, who I love lots and would not change for the world? Stop crying, be strong and call me if you need me".

Love you lots and give Lew a big kiss 4me.xXx

I NEVER FELT

I BELONGED.

I WAS

ALWAYS AN OUTSIDER

Ethel Waters

My Likkle Self & That Smile

Mum and Me '2011

Older Brother and Me

My Sister and Me '2011

CHAPTER 10: 12.01.2012

Today is a day that will forever be more significant than any other, not just because it was my thirty-first birthday! Never in a million years did I expect that from this birthday onwards it would be the day a family member died too! Someone who I had spent the last ten years getting to know, built a close bond with and who I enjoyed spending time with and will forever miss.

Friday 6th Jan '2012: I woke up just after 8:00am and I had received a call from 'K' calling to see how I was doing, what the latest was with bills, rent etc. She was ok but missing the outside world and just being free.

I let her know that I had two sisters (Dora and Donatella) moving into her room, as her room was sitting there empty and she had bills that needed clearing, including rent arrears. So, wanted to try and clear as much as possible in the hope that the council would not take back her flat while she was visiting HM Prison. Anyway by 10am the sisters had moved in with their few bits and I headed out to make my way down to Forest Hill in South-East London to visit Nan in the nursing home. I arrived, signed in and then checked to see who had been to see her and she had not had any visits in a few days.

When I got to her room, she was in bed looking into thin air. It annoys me that she is just left in silence though there is a TV I put in her room, the staff seem to forget to turn it on and I do not like it! Anyway, as always, she was happy to see me, I gave her the ginger beer that I had brought (her fav) and then asked how she was doing. After I left Nans, I headed back to West London to meet-up with Christian as he asked me to attend a Funeral Reception with him, which I did. Everyone was looking and wondering who I was apart from those who I had already been introduced to by him over the last few months. I got introduced to more people which was nice and the reception for the person who died was a great turn out too! I did not end up getting home until after 01:00 am.

Saturday 7th Jan '2012: Why was I asleep and then woken by someone ringing off the doorbell. I thought it was one of the sisters, so I looked out of the window and who was it, that joker with his lean-up-self Christian, WTF! I stormed downstairs to the front door to ask him what the hell he is doing at this time of the morning! Do you know what he said?

"Because I can, because you're my friend."

I told him to get the fuck away from the door and to take his female companion who looked like she was under the influence of some serious drugs. I was far from impressed that he had brought this person to the door, not to mention the state that he was in too at that time of the night! So, I just slammed the door and made my way back up to the flat and back to bed then ended up waking at 10:30 am, got washed and dressed, ready to pop to the Post Office. Donatella woke and when I looked in the room there was no Dora, both her sister and I started getting worried, so we called around a few of the girls from the Club and they told us that she had gone out with Claudia.

Then about 30mins later she comes through the door, telling us what an excellent night they had out raving etc. I told her she had us super worried and that she was a 'dirty stop-out' Lol. I ended up speaking to 'C' briefly and she was on a downer due to her idiot baby father upsetting her and I said:

"Try not to let him get you to vex and keep your head-up".

Monday 9th Jan '2012: I received a text from mum late afternoon telling me that Nan was in the hospital due to a urine infection. Thanks, mum for the text message, obviously I was not worthy of a phone call to tell me about Nan!!! I did not like the fact that Nan was on her own there, but I knew she was in the best place and she would be out in a few days, by God's Grace. It is something that she has been in the hospital for a few times over the years so thought nothing of it! Told mum I would go and visit her tomorrow first thing in the morning. Though I wanted to go today, I did not bother as I knew mum and the rest of them would have been going, I did not want to see my Aunt M and sure she did not want to see me either!

In all honesty, I did not want to see anyone my mum, aunt P or uncle T as I was still fuming with them all, as they had decided to STOP my Nan from having any more home visits. The family quality time (once a month), which she enjoyed and looked forward to as this was the only time, she saw outside the nursing home doors. As far as I was concerned, there was no consideration, thought, or care as to the negative impact it would have on Nans' health or mental state! I knew back in December when Nan spent her first Christmas in the ten years that she had been in a nursing home, that it was going to be her last Christmas! That look in her face when I told her that her children had decided to put an end to all home visits and leave her in the nursing home brought me to (tears) as I could see that she felt like a burden.

Nan did not want that, nor was she going to make a fuss about it either. As much as I was so mad, I tried not to show it as I did not want to make her upset; so instead, I reassured her that she would not be alone on Christmas day as I would be coming to spend it with her in the nursing home. Christmas Eve arrived and I went to see Nan and hoped I would have been able to stay but the nursing home policy did not allow it but thank god I had my good friend aka 'birthday twin' Dion living down the road in Sydenham. I called letting her know my dilemma and asked if I could stay over at hers which was fine, so I was able to wake up Christmas day stroll up the road to spend it with Nan till 18:00 then went back to my friends. I was so, so grateful even though I did not want to call her or anyone during that time of the year asking them if I can stay at their home because going to mums certainly was not an option!

But I called Di and will forever be grateful. Thank you again. x

It had only been three months prior (October) that Nan had lost her brother. I believe his spirit may have been calling her to join him, even more, as he would be able to see that she was all alone! I am sure he too would have been heartbroken to see her monthly home visits had stopped; this **(in my eyes**) would make anyone not want to carry on living! I had hoped that Nan would not be going anywhere soon because she still had her wits about her, though unable to do for herself except feed herself.

Nan knew I would always come to visit her no matter what, maybe she also felt like a burden where I was concerned, knowing that I no longer lived down the road. But that could not have been further from the truth; she was the only reason for my regular visits to South-East London; otherwise, there would have been no reason to make so many trips. #SouthWasStress

Briefly, during the summer of this year, I met someone while up in the Westend at an audition, which Christian attended with me and it was him who informed me that this person liked me and wanted to talk! I did not know who he was at first until a week or so later when he invited me to his home and saw his music on his wall! He is a well-known UK artist who I remember from back-in-the-day between 2004-2006, an accomplished songwriter, entrepreneur, and voice actor. It was a brief and casual thing, were still in contact now and again via the odd exchange of texts to see how were doing!

Tuesday 10th Jan '2012: I got up and made my way down to Kings College hospital, Nan was in bed all smiles and happy to see me. I stayed for a couple of hours; told her I would be back tomorrow as I would not be coming on Thursday as it was my birthday. I saw my older brother Del, there too and others started to arrive, so I left and made my way back to Shepherd's Bush. The next day (Wednesday) I went down to see Nan again and spend time with her, she was in bed and was her usual self. Talking and then laying just staring at me, as she does! I stayed a few hours and reminded her that I would see her on Friday instead of tomorrow, kissed her goodbye and left.

Thursday 12th Jan '2012: I was woken up just after 09:00am by a phone call from my uncle telling me Nan had not long died! I could not believe what I was hearing, I had only seen her yesterday and she was fine. Plus, today of all days, she has died, wow, in shock! Straight away something in me said that she waited till this day 'my birthday' to pass over! It felt like it was a sign from her saying sorry for the way she treated me in the past plus to let me know that she loved me. It was her only significant way to say (sorry, goodbye and I love you) on my **Thirty-First Birthday**.

Though I was shocked, upset, and sad, it did not hit me as bad as I thought it would have, because deep down I already knew that she was ready to go from Christmas day when she spent her last Xmas not surrounded by family but in the nursing home. I know Nan's final connection with me was her dying on my birthday that was her one and only gift to me which I received loud and clear, thank you. x - So sorry Nan, that I was not with you during your last moments!

Monday 16th Jan '2012: Today has been an exceptionally low one, been at home all day and when I woke this morning the gas had run out and the emergency had all been used too, KMT! I asked the 'sisters' if they have a spare £10 until tomorrow, but they are just as broke as me, so no heating or hot water and outside is 'cutting' (cold) like it is going to snow. I cried today as I listened to music while thinking about Nanny. Spoke to my older brother Del who was trying to sell his things in the flat before he gets kicked out while still insisting that he is not going to nans' funeral. I know his hurting from the way, Aunty M spoke to him on Tuesday when he visited nanny in the hospital.

He then told me how mummy and aunty Pet was chatting about me on Christmas day due to me choosing to spend it with Nan at the nursing home, Kmt! I feel so low, sad, lonely, and thinking about how 'TD' (Turkish Delight) is doing, and I sent him a text. I also exchanged a few text messages with 'SK'. 'K' called to tell me she just finished watching me on TV in **'Saints and Scroungers'** so did Simon (Richards brother) call to say he just saw me on TV, Lol. Also spoke to Eleanor, Charl's, Dion and Tasha.

Friday 20th Jan '2012: Its Nan's nine-nights this evening! *Nine-Nights, also known as Dead Yard, is a funerary tradition practised in the Caribbean (primarily Jamaica, Grenada, Belize, Dominica, Barbados, Guyana, Trinidad, Haiti, and the Dominican Republic). It is what you would call an extended wake that lasts for several days, with roots in African religious tradition.*

Thursday 2nd Feb '2012: Nan's funeral and no-show of my older brother. I cannot get my head around why he did not attend the burial of our Nan, the person who loved and adored him. She was the one he lived with from pre-school to late teens. Maybe Aunty M told him not to show his face, as I know they exchanged words, but even if that were the case, how could he allow anyone to keep him away from saying his final goodbyes!

I cannot believe she is gone, miss her so much, it was a lovely send-off. I was surprised that they (her children) did not get her a horse and cart as she grew up riding horses back home in Jamaica. But now she has finally been laid to rest and buried in Grove Park cemetery; no more nursing home visits only graveside from here onwards! The months of Jan & Feb was an upsetting, low, high with mixed emotions having had Nan die on my birthday and then buried in February. A time I knew would come one day but hoped and prayed that she would have many more years in her, but this was not the case.

Nan is the third grandparent to have died, I was not even fortunate enough to have any children and (if I do) they will not get to meet their great-grandparents which is a big shame. On a spiritual level, I can only hope that if I am destined to have children maybe my grandparents have already met them! There taking care of them until it is their time to arrive in my life and if I am meant to have any, then I am sure like my Grandma and Granddad Nan will get to meet them before me anyway. I pray and hope to meet all grandparents again one day! Thank you, Nan, aka Mama D. x

As the year drew closer to the end and the Christmas time was approaching, I knew that I did not want to spend it in London as all I could think about was my last Christmas spent with Nan in the nursing home and how my Christmases would not be the same again until I have my own family, by god's grace. So, I decided to ask my friend who is a Photographer named Chase from the USA if I could come over, hoping that he was still living in Miami, but he was now in Washington DC, which was still ok with me as I just knew I wanted to get away!

Sunday 23rd Dec '2012: I flew out to Washington on my favourite airline (Virgin Atlantic) and was picked up by Chase, his brother JJ and his girlfriend, Saphan. I would be staying with them all, which at the time I did not know it was his brothers' girlfriends' home which was a lovely house located in Maryland. Later that night after chilling, eating, and smoking, I had a minor 'anxiety attack' asking myself why I just flew out to the states on my own, what if something happened to me etc!

I ended up going up to the room and called one of my friends so I could hear a familiar voice and then I calmed down and pulled myself together, LMFAO! The next day I was indoors a few hours by myself while everyone else had popped out. While looking around at some of the pictures of Saphan's family, I noticed a beautiful cabinet with records and a photo of a handsome man who looked like a singer.

Then I saw the name, Wilson Pickett. So (as you do) I took out my phone and googled his name and could not believe what I was reading, this man was LEGENDARY.

Wilson Pickett *(18th Mar 1941 – 19th Jan 2006) was an American singer and songwriter from 1955-2006.*

As I continued to research him, I saw a photo of Saphan and realised she was his youngest child.

The fourth generation born and raised in Englewood, NJ, Saphan Pickett is the youngest daughter of Soul Legend, Wilson Pickett Jr.

Like WOW, I was staying in the home of this legendary man's daughter and she was so humble, down to earth, and welcoming. What is the likelihood of that, to start of the year of 2012 with a loss on my birthday (R.I.P) Nan, then end it in the home of a daughter whose father is Wilson Pickett!

Below is a note I made at the back of my diary regarding the number 12 during this year of '2012.

- 12yrs worth of written diaries.

- 12yrs I have been Independent on my own.

- 12, is the door number. of the studio flat I am currently renting.

- 12th Jan, my birthday, and the day my beautiful Nan died.

- 12th mth of the year (December) got away for Christmas and the new year.

- 12yrs since my first/last serious boyfriend and girlfriend relationship of 3 & a half years.

- Six years since I last saw Chase in '2006 when I flew out to Miami. Plus, six years since Saphan's Dad (Wilson Pickett) died = 12

- '2020, I realised the door number 84 (8 + 4) = 12. This is the home I hope to buy one day. Amen

It was an honour to have met and stayed with Saphan for those two weeks, thank you for welcoming me into your home!

Thank you, Chase, for inviting me over, it is a year that started on a low and ended on a remarkable high. To nan thank you for the ten years that I got to know and get close to you along with your farewell gift of dying on my birthday.

A 2-in-1 celebration of life to cherish each year. Love and miss you always and forever.

Legendary Wilson Pickett Cabinet

Soul Ain't nothing But A Feeling

Wilson Pickett

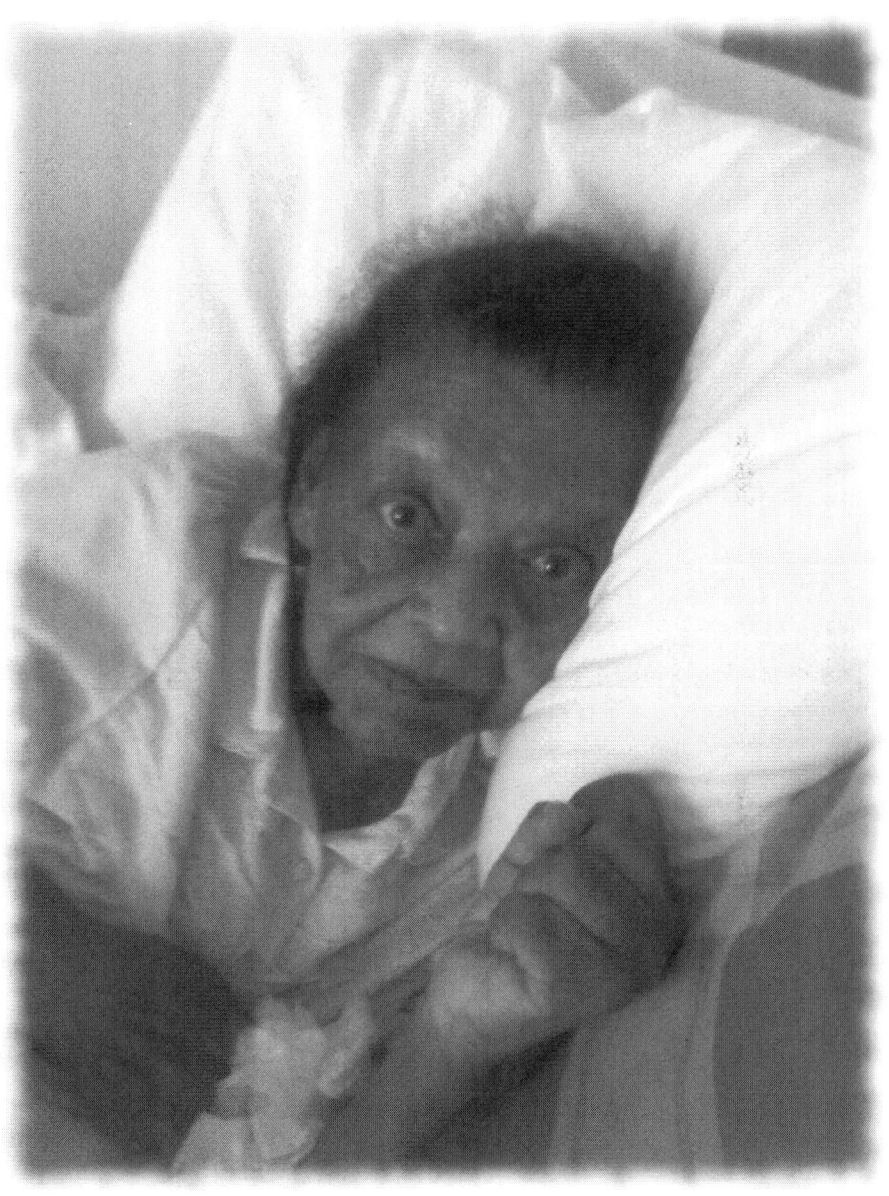

Nan (gazing at me) Like She Always Did!

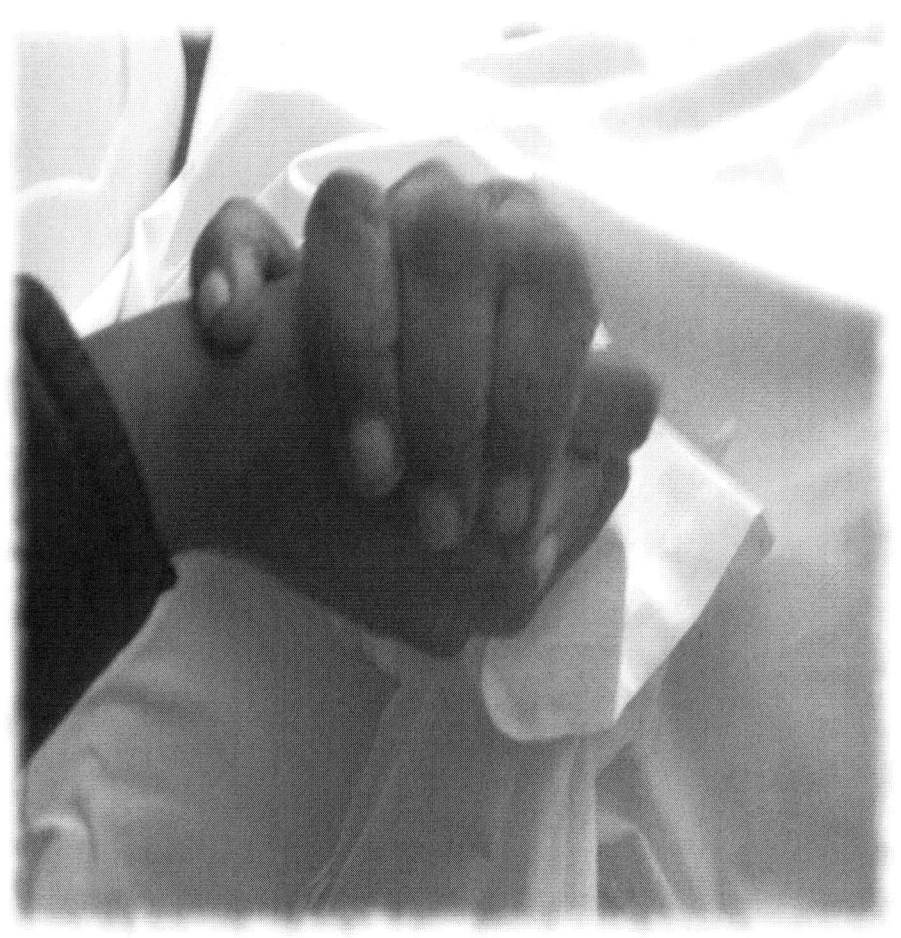

My final Goodbye... 12.01.2011. Viewing nan's body in the hospital –
Wish I had held her hand more when she was alive!

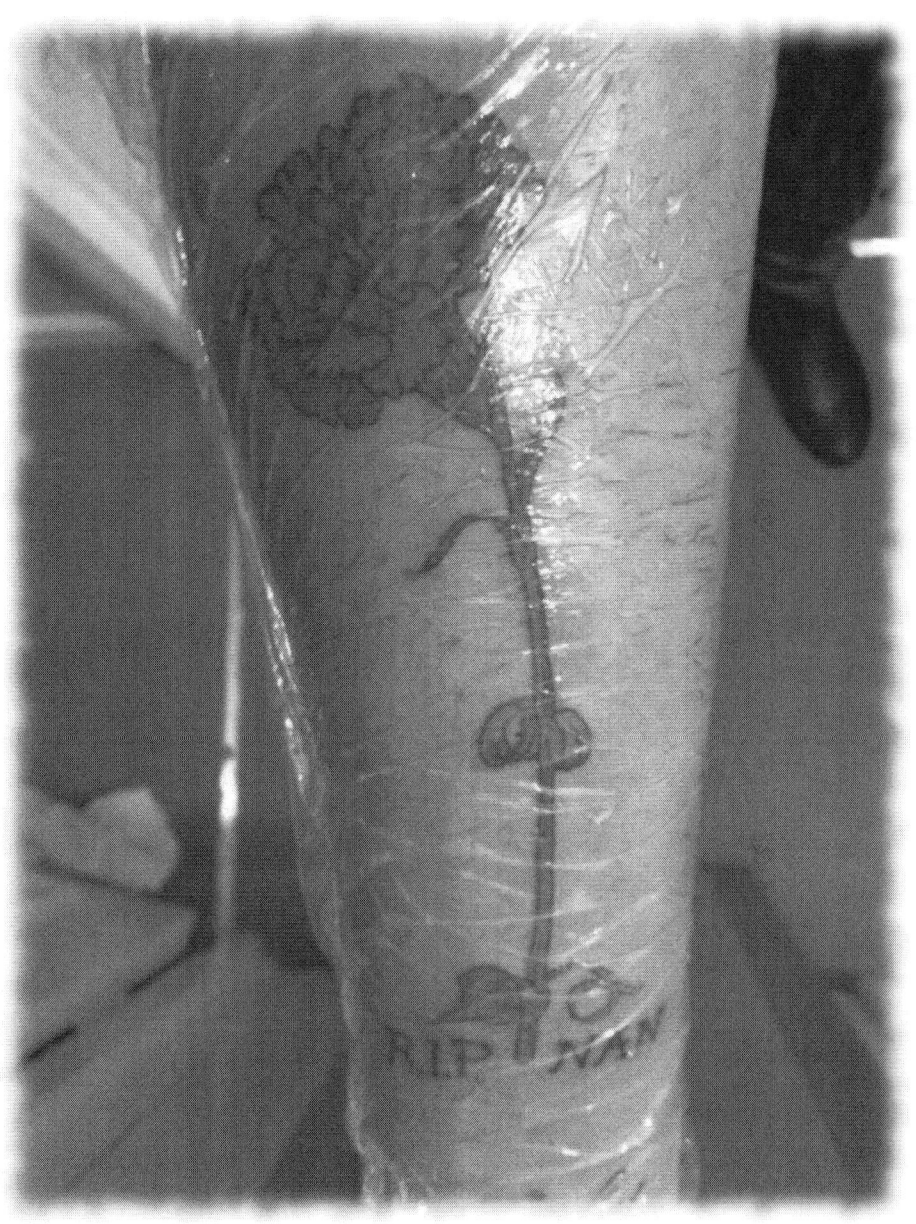

Dedicated to Nan

Photos used in Nan Eulogy

Great-Granddad and his daughter my Nan

(Mums' Jamaican and Jewish side)

CHAPTER 11: DIFFERENT FATHER, SAME MOTHER

Catford is in South-East London and I moved there in 1993. It had become the second-longest place that I had lived in, having already moved homes four times within the 11yrs of living in that area. I ended up leaving Catford for the first time in '2004 due to toxic family dramas (mum and ex-stepdad), then on Saturday 1st May '2010 marked one year since I returned to the endz!

This time I had moved directly on the main busy high street living on top of the well-known club/restaurant called Motown Soul Bar. A neighbour who I knew was living next door, that person was my older brother Del. He is four years older than me; born in April '1977. We have the same mum but different fathers though he always referred to mine as his own which I (hated) because as far as I was concerned my Dad was mine only!

Dad referred to him as his son, which in all honesty, was rightly so! Because my brother was present in my parents' life before I came along, but when I was younger, I did not see it like that and did not like hearing my brother refer to my dad as his Dad too! Do I know much about my brothers' father (not really) only what I heard come from my Nan, mum, aunt, and uncle's mouth on a regular which was?

"He is a mad man who went off his head and is in and out of Maudsley Hospital."

The words *"you're mad like your Dad"* is something that was said to my brother, which brings me to an upsetting memory that he recalls from his childhood. He mentioned it to me a few times, I would say it is a form of mental abuse because it is something that has stayed with him all his life and on his mental state. Once he told me about a time when he was a young boy, he was out in the car with our Uncle T and Aunt M, then he recalled they had spotted his Dad on the road and said to him,

"Look Del, there's your mad Dad."

They started laughing. Who does that please! Can you imagine how he felt hearing them say that to him, these two (grown arse) adults who should have known better but instead were humiliating his father while crushing their nephew's feelings and emotions too! I feel bad knowing that sometimes when my brother and I would argue or fight I would repeat the exact words about his Dad being <u>mad</u> because I knew he did not like it. Then he would call me buckteeth and other names! It is not right, but that is what children do; copy what they grow up around and that was no different for me.

I apologise for any hurt I caused him back then! Does he have a relationship with either aunt or uncle, no he does not! Could my brothers' upbringing be the reason he has never really grown-up, I say this because of him being like Peter Pan, a man on the outside but a child inside.

The only difference is there is not much happiness that he has encountered, he needs to sit down with someone (counselling) and off-load all that he has built up inside over the years! Maybe this would include having answerers from our mum who has never taken the time to know and understand him.

He lacked more love and affection than I did due to not living with mum, maybe if she explained to him; her (firstborn) why she chose to leave him in the full-time care with Nan instead of keeping him with her as she did with me! Between the both of us I have always been the more mature and responsible one. Maybe it is a female thing! While he has suffered in silence mostly keeping the way he feels, to himself (like most men) too proud to admit his hurting. Which does not help with his depression, struggling with dyslexia, feeling unloved and not wanted plus many other underlining matters which he has never spoken to me about, but I see through him!

I will never understand how you can be a parent and not care about your child — going days, weeks, months, and years without having any contact with them or knowing if their safe and alive. More so the mother because they are the carriers of life, they are the first ones to bond with their child from them growing in their belly until they give birth and finally get to meet the life that God has blessed her with; motherhood!

The moment you become a parent, it is for life, not a moment, or until they reach eighteen into adulthood that you wash-your-hands-of-them and leave them to it when the truth is **no child** asks to be born. Instead, I would rather a child be given a chance of life by being adopted or taken into care rather than not being born at all! One feature that my brother and I share with mum, though she had hers (removed) we cannot hide it.

It is like our life journey is carried as 'bags' under our eyes! Mine vary because sometimes they can be very noticeable like my brothers then other times, I do not notice them when I look in the mirror. It is something that we've both had to accept is part of our face; would I get the loose skin under my eyes removed, no, it is not that deep! Guys have complimented me over the years about my eyes and the first thought that popped into my head is.

"Really, can you not see my baggy eyes."

I may have 'bags', but in general I like my brown eyes. Even more, my eyelashes as they are naturally long and beautiful with the added help of L'Oréal Mascara. The only product that I use on my eyes. I love how flawless they look when it is applied. Females compliment me about my lashes all the time and ask, *"are they real"*. I do not do fake lashes. If I did wear them then it would only be for a photo-shoot or something like that otherwise their mine alone! Everyone's upbringing varies, which impacts on how or who you develop into once you hit adulthood. Only you can take responsibility for any choices made in your life, no one else! My older brothers' behaviour in relationships has left me feeling furious majority of the time due to him belittling them and being abusive, both mental and physical. I do not like, agree, or want to see any form of abuse even more so by a man to a female!

His past partners knew that I would get so mad whenever they informed my mum or me about the way he was treating them; it made my blood boil every time. I am not trying to make any excuses for him, but I believe his childhood experiences are partly to blame for how he is when in a relationship, but it does not make it right! Unfortunately, like many boys, he never had a father figure to look up to, learn from or get advice about females along with the rest! A father is the crucial role model who is supposed to teach their son all there is to know about becoming a man. Our uncle certainly was not a man to look up too; all he did was mistreat my brother (mentally, physically, and emotionally). This email from my brother says it all.

"Uncle T was a cunt to me when I was little; he was evil. The things he did to me he would have never done to you because he knew you had a Dad and no one deer mess with him dem days. Only Nan would save me from him sometimes! I remember he killed Baba's (Aunt M's nickname) kittens by drowning them and tying them in a black bag and throwing them in the shoot (bin)"

I know my uncle was wicked but do not know the extent of his treatment towards him. I remember there were times when he would make us stand up facing the wall with books on our head for ages, as punishment and if they fell off, he would beat us! He was one of those people who you would have to <u>catch in the act</u> to believe the way he treated (us) his niece and nephew as he was so good at covering his tracks. I would hate to think what else he did to my brother as a child! Aunty M was strict, she was the one who taught me how to tell the time. I would not be able to move from the table until I got it right, no number of tears helped either!

The odd 'slap' I received over the years from her was ok but, it was (the look) a **'don't let me slap you'** glance that was no joke, and we would know to stop whatever we were doing.

Though I looked up to her as a big sister and mum, it was moments like this where I loathed my aunt. As for my brother, whatever terrible times he encountered from living under Nans' roof with our uncle, he was lucky he got to escape for a while by going out to play with his friends. Aunty M was firm, she took no rubbish and was loving, which is what I admired about her – she was my role model! Our Uncle T was cold, sneaky with not much tolerance for us, kids. Nan was far from the 'saint' grandparent so her lying at times was nothing new. I think because my brother was my Nans' favourite she disliked whenever I stayed over because we would be having fun even though we argued and fought like cat and dog!

We still had some excellent sibling quality time together where we would be laughing, playing, and doing as kids do, but Nan hated hearing us enjoying ourselves so the best way to 'mash-it up' would be to split us up! How would she do that? By purposely making up Nuff noise 'cussing and yelling after us so that it would wake up her son (uncle T) who would then rush downstairs vex, annoyed and mad due to having his sleep disturbed! He would get up in our faces saying.

"Why are you making Nanny shout, why you not listening."

While saying this, he would either be poking or flicking us in our head. Then he would march one of us up the stairs to the fourth floor (by the ear) to sit on the stairs outside his room until told otherwise — a sneaky person who took the living piss all the years that he lived under nans roof!

The man would take nans' alcohol, drink it off and fill it up with water then put it back as if he had never touched it until she realised and would cuss bad words! I suppose this was clear evidence that back in the eighties, he had a drinking problem that again was brushed under the carpet as if there was no problem! #YerrRight

The only good memory shared with my uncle is the love of music along with his passion for making Lamp Shades! Music was his I am 'awake' alarm blasting tunes from his bedroom with his door wide open for us all to hear. So, whenever either or both aunts were home, along with mum, sometimes they would all be in his room listening to music while having their 'big people' conversations. He would be sat in his chair while they sat on the edge of his bed, including me at times and we would all be (rocking) back and forward to the music, LMFAO!

It may sound weird but what can I say this was something that we did while enjoying the music and talking, instead of sitting still. So, we not only danced at times, but we were 'rockers' too.

My brother was the only one who did not participate in this! Growing up in a dysfunctional family is the reason to this day why he still has no closure. Why he decided to remove himself from everyone, all the way up to Wales because our Forbes family take no responsibility for any of their actions, instead they live in denial. Had uncle T, not taken it upon himself to **OPEN** his <u>big mouth</u> having promised his older sister (my mum) that he would not say anything but did! It did not surprise me, but I was still mad, disappointed, and upset for my brother because he confided in our mum who then confided in me, knowing she could tell me anything.

I kept what mum told me, to myself though I wanted to tell my Aunt M, I was not about to cause any stress to her or the unborn baby. I never expected mum to tell her brother (our Uncle T) knowing that he had asked her not to say anything, but unfortunately mum had no loyalty

of <u>silence</u> to her child! So, when it all blew up, it was the final straw for me, and I knew I needed to break free by removing myself from them all!

Between my brother and I even though we have different fathers, we resemble one another and have a lot in common too from our childhood.

But he is lucky that God has blessed him with three children (two girls and a boy) from two different woman. I hope that one day he will turn his life around and make them proud.

THE BAGS

UNDER MY EYES

ARE HEREDITARY

THEIR APART OF

ME AND

TELL A STORY

Anikka Forbes

North Peckham Estate Days in the 80's

North Peckham Estate Days in the 80's

CHAPTER 12: #SWSWIB

F riday 29th April '2011, the day I moved to West London, since then whenever people ask me *"why did you leave south"* my motto has always been because.

South was Stress... West is Blessed

The last thirty years of my life was in South-East London, having moved postcodes a total of 12 times, before deciding to leave South-London behind and start anew in West London. I was born and bred right on the notorious North Peckham Estate. *North Peckham consisting mainly of high-rise flats and was heavily redeveloped in the 1960s.*

I have always felt an affinity towards someone much younger than me who was starting life within my old community. The estate had a £290 million regeneration in the late 1990s and early 2000s, then it gained nationwide notoriety in the media when 10-year-old **Damilola Taylor** from Nigeria was stabbed to death on 27th November 2000. Strange as it sounds, I have felt a bond between us, probably because of him living on the same estate and attending the same Primary School (as me) called Oliver Goldsmith. Till this day I can remember as clear as day when I heard it on the news and was sickened, devastated, but most of all, my heart went out to his family.

I ended up moving back in '2005, to Peckham for a year to stay at my Nan's new house located on Sumner Rd, having been re-housed from the North-Peckham Estate a few years prior. I only moved there due to staying in my nieces' room at my sister-in-law's home while she shared with her mum, on a temporary basis. Having been occupying it for just under or over a year, it was time to give my niece back her space! So, moved back to Peckham for a while as I knew Nans room was sitting there empty due to her being nursing home bound, plus I was driving, so getting about was no issue! My uncle was still living there, and I figured that staying there for a while would help me to save, but the moment I moved in and saw how he was keeping the house plus how much of Nans' ornaments and personal items were missing; I knew from then, there was going to be <u>dramas</u>!

That is a whole other story; for the trilogy that I want to create by writing book 2 and 3! Family can sometimes be your worst enemy, so much that they end up driving you away; in my case, I did what many would not do; **removed myself**! It was back in February '2011 when I said to myself.

"Fuck it... I need to start putting me first, by taking
My self away from all the toxic and negativity that was everywhere
I turned from the moment I stepped out of my door".

Certain people, I could not stand to see anymore, while feeling like the family drama was drowning me and regretted moving back to be closer to them when they were the ones pushing me away. I knew it was time to pack-up and leave South-East London to an area that I did not know and where no one knew me!

I visited my old-school friend 'K', who is originally from south but now living in West London, she knew I was thinking about leaving Catford. Which is when she invited me to stay with her until I sorted out somewhere to rent, which seemed like a great idea so took her up on her offer. Living in a 2-bedroom flat; therefore, no spare room for me, only the sofa in the living-room to sleep on, which was not a problem, I adapt to change! Living with a single mum and her five-year-old daughter may not be everyone's cup of tea, but I could not wait to be living with a <u>little person</u> again having not done so since '2000 when I lived with my little sister and baby brother.

I adore kids, plus wanted time out from living by myself! A roof over my head, in a new area where I knew only her; I would be giving her regular weekly rent and would also be at hand whenever she needed a babysitter, so it was a win, win situation for us both. There were only two other people that I knew in West London, but they were absent from my life, my Dad and step-mum. It had been years since I had last been to their house, was not even sure of the door number as I had thought about paying them a surprise visit. But in all honesty, this was unlikely, because at the time I did not care how close I might be to him, having not spoken or seen him since 2008, prior to seeing him at my birthday party back in Jan '2011.

Why? Due to him telling me something I <u>never expected</u>, over the phone which should have been said to me in person, nevertheless, I was far from happy! But for me to get my head around the news and believe it, I gave him an ultimatum. To arrange a meeting or I would have nothing more to say to him, for the simple fact that I would have been 'none-the-wiser' had he not told me in the first place! But he did tell me and chose to do nothing about it, which left me disappointed, upset, angry, let down and a whole other bunch of emotions. The main thing that pissed-me-off was the fact that he did not take me seriously! I believe

"Actions speak louder than words"

I did what I said I would, cut-off all contact which was no biggie really as he has been an absent not present Dad for most of my life with no contact for years on end. So, it was nothing new, not seeing or speaking to him, the fact that I was moving not too far from him did not matter. Moving in with my friend was all I focused on. As I am writing this, I can reflect; I believe the rejection received from a young age, reflects on my actions in trying to understand or see if someone is genuine. I am a patient person, but if I feel like I am giving you my all then at some point, I start feeling like my company, calls etc. is not being appreciated then I end up drifting away or put an end to any more of my precious time by locking-off the person (block and delete).

The same way how I might say or do something to test someone's' reaction, to see if they care or not is something that I do to protect myself, it shows me if a person is genuine, sometimes without even knowing that I am doing it!

Before up and moving to Shepherds Bush, I was back living in Catford on the high-street, above the well-known Motown and the owner was also my landlord. Motown was a popular place that was graced by a few celebrities over the decades alongside many regulars too! I was an occasional raver there who also enjoyed the food and the music! I had heard that he had a two-bed flat above his club that was sitting empty, so I jumped at the chance of asking him if I could rent it. I was ready (after 4years) to relocate back to where my mum, Nan and aunts all lived having been living in Penge, for the third time renting a studio flat. Plus, the bonus of another family member already residing above Motown, my brother was great too! Both living side by side next door to each other for the first time as neighbours. Lol!

The fresh New Year had just started, my birthday 12th January had just come and gone, then Saturday 29th (two weeks later) I would be having a belated house-party at my mums to celebrate my new era of turning 'thirty'. I was looking forward to having it and could not wait! Plus, it seemed like '2011 was my *'year to be seen'* having had four friends contact me to ask what I was doing on television as they were sat at home watching me on their TV in **'Saints and Scroungers'** as mentioned in Chapter 10.

In a few days, I would finally be starting the basic Clothes Making Class, something that I had an interest in for a while! When I was not working, at the gym or learning a new skill, I was at home on my laptop doing my usual Networking on Social Media or putting myself forward for Castings. Not forgetting the company of my four fluffy-longhaired babies (my cats) named, Biscuit, Mix-up, Cookie and Cheeky. Yes, they looked like their name! There was also someone new in my life, who just like (TD) we met via Facebook. He is officially the first man via my second FB account **Nicky Forbes** who I met, dated briefly, and grew close too!

I refer to him as 'Merlz' though his actual name is Merlin. Our first communication came from him being interested in finding out more about me, having seen and complimenting some of my modelling photos, which led to continued messaging via FB before we decided to exchange numbers. The wickedest thing is that it was only a few weeks before my birthday party that he came into contact with me, so my brazen self-thought the perfect first meet would be to invite him to my birthday party. I thought he was polite when he accepted my invite, but I still did not expect him to attend, but he did, so that was a lovely added addition to my night.

There 'Merlz' was standing at the front-door looking sharp, handsome, dapper, and fine (if I do) say so myself!!! He handed me a bottle of champs along with a big hug which was well-received, and I welcomed him into my party. I was so proud of my Dad being among the rest of my family and friends I introduced them both, which for me was a big deal!

Nothing more attractive to me than a man who has his shit-on-lock and who is ambitious plus I admired his love for music and the industry in general. He loved being in his studio playing or making music direct at his apartment in Croydon, which was at the top so had a fabulous view of London. I remember the first time he invited me to his place it was so relaxing, chilled and I enjoyed listening to some of his work (music) while also catching Nuff jokes with his friends. I recall one of his female friends talking in general and then got on to a topic about <u>negative</u> people and how she has no interest in being around them, something I could identify with one hundred per cent! Once everyone had left, we were alone and able to continue getting to know each other by asking questions as you do.

Merlz ticked all the boxes except for the main vital one, which has always been a no-go zone for me, **men with children.** A proud father and a great role-model. My preference was a man who was not a parent so that we could go through the whole amazing and fantastic pregnancy experience, together for the first time! The fact that he had kids did not impact on how much I liked him 💋 or how much we had in common and connected. So took each day as it came by not thinking too deep or far ahead (if only) Lol!

It was early to mid-February that I had finally made up my mind to leave Catford South-East London and move to West London, though it was not the best time for me to up and move due to being broke till payday. Nor did it help that I had my mum stressing me about money I owed her, so much so that on Monday 28th she sent me a text saying.

MUM: *"When are you going to pay back the money you owe me"?*

ME: *"Soon as I get paid, as I am broke right now and on emergency for my Gas and Electric."*

MUM: *"You are leaving me in debt."*

ME: *"You're not the only one in debt, plus I have to move, so I need to sort that out."*

She did not even bother asking when or where I was moving to or if I needed help packing, nothing! But this is **standard procedure** for mum not to care about me, yet she would continuously call or text going on about the money lent to me and when am I going to pay it back. When you cannot even borrow or rely on your parents for help, you learn fast that the only person in life you can count on is yourself even when you do not have much and struggling! Thank God, for always seeing me through. Amen

Tuesday 1st March' 2011, it is Nans' eighty-third birthday, but I was not feeling too well as my stomach (as usual) was playing up. I received a text from my Boo asking how I was, I told him I was home feeling a little unwell and he told me to come to his so he could look after me. Even though he was busy - how lovely is he! So, I got sorted out, packed a few clothes (just in case), and made my way to see my Nan when I received a text from mum asking.

"Have you called to wish your Nan Happy Birthday."

Really! I thought. I did not even bother reply, she is a joker to be asking me that question. Why would I be calling, it is her birthday, and she is in the nursing home alone, so like I do nearly every day I am going to see her. Kmt! After spending some quality time with Nan, I made my way up to Croydon to relax and be looked after by Mr Music Lover. I ended up spending a few days with him and it was GREAT! He surprised me when he introduced me to one of his friends, as his girlfriend, I did not expect that, but most def was not complaining! I was made to feel right at home, well looked after and content. Thank you, Merlz.x

But unfortunately, the unexpected happened! Within the space of a week and a half, he had lost his Nan, something that no one could have predicted, then an additional loss which was unbelievable and made big headline news. An iconic old school British Reggae Artist, who I grew up listening to due to my Dad's love for his music and he also knew him personally too! Little did I know it was Merlin's beloved uncle. I could not believe it – SHOCKED.com

Tuesday 15th March '2011, David Victor Emmanuel aka **Smiley Culture** died, but I, like many others, could not/did not believe he took his own life and knowing that there are corrupt police in the world it just did not sit right with me and it did not add up. Only God knows the truth! Just like the death of the English Rose 'Princess Diana, do I believe that was an accident? Neither of these deaths (in my eyes) was an accident. #MyOpinion #YerISaidIt #GodAintSleeping

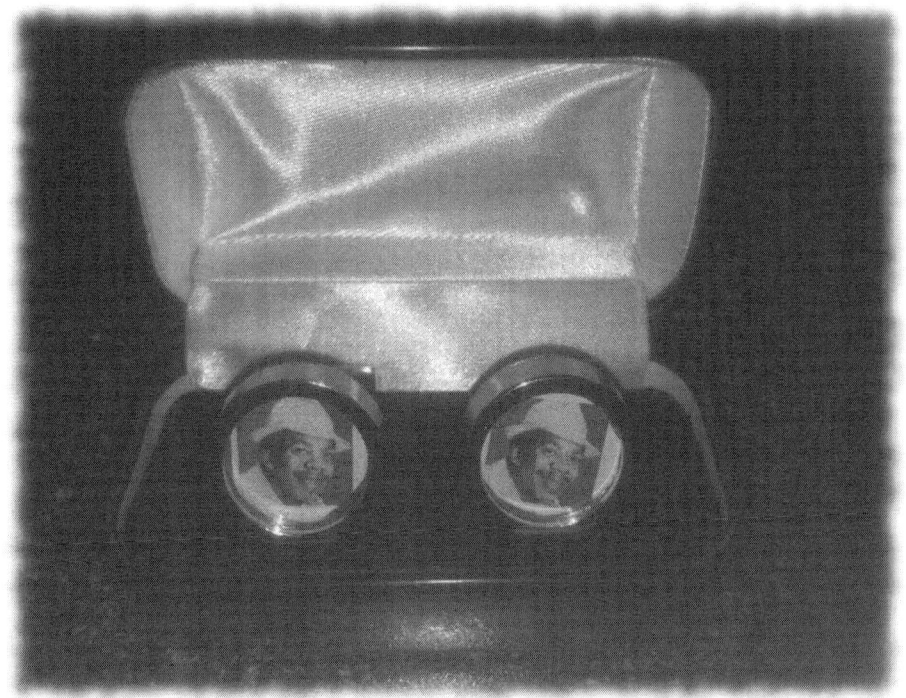

1st Ever Cufflinks Present Given.

I tried as best as I could to be there and supportive, but as you can imagine it was a rollercoaster time for him, so I had to be extra patient and understanding which I am more than capable of doing and more! All these qualities naturally lie within me, though it was hard for me at times when I tried calling to see how he was or wanted to see him, so I could wrap my arms around him and let him know I was there whenever he needed me.

I made sure to be there when it mattered by attending the community committee meeting because he needed all the support he could get although, he had his family and others, I too wanted to be his support. I took part in the big March for Justice which started from Wandsworth to Scotland Yard. Smiley would have been proud of the turn out on that day from his family, friends, and fans.

None of us knows what is around the corner and how quickly things can change in a flash. I went from turning thirty, to having a fabulous house party after weeks of pleading with my mum to let me have it at hers. Dad made sure he attended having not seen him in over five years, thanks to my Uncle K (Dad's brother). Without a doubt, Dads' presence was what made the start of my new era even greater. I know my mum was more shocked to see him at my party, so-much-so that she tried to pretend like she did not recognise him! I took as many pictures as possible on my night. An authentic memorabilia person I am, and nothing beats looking back on past photos or videos which I have and cherish from years ago. But there is one photo of that night taken on my camera by someone else of me standing with both my parents, honestly the pic speaks a thousand words, i.e.

"If looks could kill"

Either my Dad, myself, or both of us would be (brown bread) dead! Mums' facial expression while looking at us both was not a good look and saddens me that whatever thought she had at that moment was not a positive one.

Not everyone that I invited attended my belated birthday party, but I believe.

"Those who made it were the ones who were meant to be present and those that did not attend, weren't meant to be there".

Like my Aunt M who I invited but was a no show, that was her own choice! Even though I knew she would not have attended anyway as, by this time, we were no longer speaking due to her *'deleting me from her life'*. In truth, I was not on good speaking terms with my mum either, leading up to my birthday party. Because as mentioned in Chapter 10, Mum and the rest had stopped Nans once a month, rotational visits from the nursing home to their homes and I could not believe it.

There was no consideration for what Nan wanted or how it would affect her mental and emotional health. Her one day of quality time with the family, taken away. How could they think it was ok to leave their mum in a nursing home without any home visits? What did they think was going to happen! How did they think she was going to feel? Like a burden!

None of them were regular visitors; no one knew how much longer my Nan would be around, so they should have taken that into account by not changing her routine. Nope, not them! You would have thought that Nan being so close at first (nursing home in Catford) would mean regular visits from her children and other grandchildren, but that was not the case which would make me so vex. So, when Nan had to move to a new one in Sydenham due to her current nursing home closing down. It was no longer 10mins away, but now a 30-45mins journey which I knew would result in even more fewer visits from the family. I would always check when <u>signing in the visitors' book</u> to see who and when anyone had last visited.

Majority of the time, I was appalled by her being left days on end without a visit, except for me, but not surprised! Even my move to West London did not stop me from jumping on public transport back to South-East to see Nan. I was always worried about her feeling lonely or forgotten about in the nursing home. So made sure I took control by making regular visits, keeping her company, bringing her favourite treats, asking her what she was thinking/feeling and about her past. Most of all, she received plenty of love and affection from me. As mentioned, prior, I am passionate about memorabilia, so the recordings I have with Nan, either at the nursing home or with the family are all precious.

More so once her home visits had ended 'hand on heart' I felt it would only be a matter of time that she would either start to decrease or simply give-up. An elderly person needs (just like a child) time, care, and love and if you subject them to just looking at the same four walls every day this is not going to help only make things worse. Nan had a tv in her room, which I put there otherwise she would be in silence, though sometimes I would visit her, and she was just left lying-in bed staring into thin air without the TV on and it broke my heart. I treasured every moment spent with her during her nursing home days, though I have not been able to bring myself to watch much footage as her loss is still a little raw for me. I have a photo of her on my wardrobe just staring at me, something she did a lot whenever I visited her. I would be talking (as I do) while she would be gazing at me then I would ask her.

ME: "*What are you thinking, Nan*"

and she would always say.

NAN: *"Nothing"*

While continuing to look at me. Deep down I believe and even Christian once said the same thing to me during a conversation about her, that maybe she was saying to herself *'how sorry she was for the way she treated me'* when I was a young child!

Though I wanted to, I never did have the conversation with her, as I did not want to upset her. Her eyes when staring at me were of someone who was deeply sorry for the wicked treatment, she (dealt me) in my younger years. A person's eyes speak volumes and I saw through hers a few times whenever she was looking deep at me to the point where it was like she was saying.

> ***"I can't believe out of everyone, it is you Nicky, who is the one that is always coming to see me".***

When she was first in the Catford nursing home I was the one who would get her wheelchair and take her out for a stroll down the road; I was the one who saw that she had not been taken care of properly when I saw marks and bruises on her, having had one of the staff inform me that she had a fall. I was livid and worried at not knowing my Nan's treatment behind closed doors.

I spoke to the staff that were meant to be caring for her took photos of her bruises and was horrified when I got home and looked back on them. Which is when I thought this neglect needed to be exposed having seen on the news the same stories, so I contacted the local newspaper, sent them the photos and they published the story. My actions made the home and staff realise I was not (one to be played with) where my Nan was concerned and was ready to tear off anyone's head who was not handling her with care. Nan only had one person looking out for her needs and wants, which was me, due to her children deciding between themselves, to stop all her home visits! Till this day it hurts, and I will never forgive them for it! Did their selfish choice affect my Nan? Yes, it did! #Fact

I learnt about her past and hard upbringing back in Jamaica something which she had never spoken about and kept locked away in her head for years. The pure innocence in her face (like a child) was heart-wrenching and shocking and then to hear the vile word **'rape'** come out of my Nan's mouth was devastating. She was raped as a girl by one of the boys that worked on her father's land. I could not believe what I was hearing!

Even spoke about the death of her first son. Truth be known, women and children back in those times were subject to sexual abuse regularly within the home or elsewhere it is an attack and violation to the bearers of life, females! Has it got any better? I think it is got worse because those paedophiles and rapist are going that extra mile by not just raping but killing too! People that commit these offences are sometimes innocent victims of the same or similar abuse, repeating the same cycle.

It is a sad, disturbing fact but does not make it right! Alzheimer's, I believe my Nan suffered from a little but nothing to be overly concerned about because she still had her faculties about her and remembered everyone's names, thank God. I was my mum and two aunties biggest fans growing up. But it was my Aunt. Me, who was my inspiration, the one who I looked up to and admired everything about her. Although she was the strictest out of the three of them, in my eyes, she was most definitely the 'strong' one, or so I thought up until my late twenties. 😒

Why, because of the ultimate family drama involving her joker and waste of space husband accused of having an affair with my older brother's girlfriend! Yep, there it is right there! The reason why my relationship with my biggest role-model, second mum, friend and beloved aunt came to an end, for those of you that (know us) and wondered. My aunt could not understand why I had not told her what I had heard from my mum (first) then my brother later shared with me what he had told our mum in confidence! Even though I tried to explain my reasons for not telling her, simply because she was pregnant; therefore, I refused to cause unnecessary stress that could have had a negative impact on her or my unborn cousin!

Otherwise, without any hesitation, I would have most definitely informed my aunt or tried to get my brother to speak to her. There was nothing that I could not or would not talk to my aunt about; I was like her little sister and she the big sister that I never had! But nope, Aunty M was not having none-of-it. So, from that point, onwards (in my eyes), she was no longer the strong *'woman in control'* who did not put up with rubbish! Especially knowing how much she always had to say when it came to my mum and her toxic relationship with my (younger siblings) Dad! Her mean and deceitful husband continued to manipulate and mentally abuse her behind closed doors. Would not be surprised if he had ever been physical towards her, it is not something I ever witnessed or heard about but who knows!

#NoOneKnowsWhatGoesOnBehindClosedDoors

I know she was not happy! As she confided in her brother (my uncle) then he would report to mum her exact words. Along with complaining about money, he always had to give/lend her; why? Because she married a seriously MEAN man! He should have tried to help his sister out of that situation; instead, he chatted her business behind her back to their older sister. But you would never hear her admit any of this then or even now, I am sure!

#WhatHappensInTheDarkAlwaysComesToLight

For me, the moment I witnessed the two actions, which I know was not her doing, but she went along with it, was the final straw for me. Then she segregated herself from the family! And when I thought she could not go any lower what did she go and do; remove my cousin (Shannon) from my mums' childcare. Why would you take your child away from her aunt (your sister) into the hands of strangers? Fucking outrageous! #JokeBusiness

Mum had been looking after her niece, Aunt M's daughter from the age of one or two years old. For me, their actions spoke a thousand words. Had there been **'no truth'** in his affair, why did he make her segregate from all of (us) the family! Hiding away, locked up at home like a stepford wife mum and godmother Kim's words, not mine! *The definition of* **'Stepford Wife'** *is a term used for someone that is so obedient and perfect that he or she seems almost like a robot.*

Here is an email between us which is amusing and surprising looking back on it now. Whereas that was not the case when I first saw it as <u>one word</u> in particular 'hurt' and saddened me to the core. Never did I expect such a 'word' to come from my aunt, who just like my mum I loved more than myself and would do anything for them both! But the line once again had been crossed to the point of no return! Below is the last email in '2010 exchanged between us. All I did was inform her that the fire alarm company called me about her house alarm. I should not have bothered!

From: Anikka Forbes
Sent: 07/12/2010, 18:02
To: Aunt M

Do not make me laugh! Me sick, far from it. You are the bigger woman, so why ya wasting your time sending an email back if you think that I am overreacting! It was a stupid thing to say, "I'll get you removed" when obviously that is what you have to do! Remember I informed you and I did not make up any issue about them contacting me, it was you. Simple!

From: Aunt M
Sent: Wed 08/12/2010, 09:51
To: Anikka

Yes, I am the bigger woman Nikki hence I have no reason to be spiteful to you; furthermore, if I felt I was wasting my time I would not have bothered to thank you in the first place, you know me, Nikki, when have I ever been spiteful to you? Besides making that comment is not spiteful so therefore you used the word in the wrong context. You are carrying on like the comment was sent with attitude well for your information as I mentioned before it was not sent with malice you just want to read into it that way. But I should not be surprised that is you all over you just like argument and had to twist a simple comment that was sent with thanks and sincerity!

We are not speaking so; obviously, you did not have to contact me, you are not the only key holder, they have other names so you could have refused. Now if you did not contact me, then that would have been spiteful, not me telling you I'll get you removed, that's all it means plain and simple, it was a text message for god sake, over-reacting that's an understatement! I said this to you a few years ago and I will repeat it now and it stops here. Forget I exist I have deleted you from my mind, so delete me from yours, you do not exist in my world!

Really, WOW, ok! Her words **deleted** me. So, I am now the (deleted one) where Aunt M is concerned! Nevertheless, I always admired and loved my mums' relationship with her sisters. Their tight bond from growing up together, unlike me and my older brother who grew up apart!

Mum is the eldest though people never believed it and Aunt M is the youngest and she was the leader of the three of them, to me anyway! My Aunt P has always been the quiet one, a little nerdy and the follower of the three. Mum and her youngest sister Aunt M were born on the same day 5th Dec, but different years 1956 and 1965. How amazing and unique is that to share the same birthday with your sibling as if they were twins.

I loved it whenever they had a joint house-party on North-Peckham Estate for their birthdays and from the tender age of three years, I was up-in-the-mix with the adults loving the tunes. There was little me sneaking among the adults watching them 'scrubbing-up' against the wall dancing.

While learning the words and enjoying all the 'Lovers Rock, Rare Groove and Revival' music as it was blasting out of the huge speakers. It was heaven! #80sNorthPeckhamEstateDays

The day I said goodbye to Catford to head to West, is the day that Prince William and Kate got married an iconic day to remember my departure. Anyway, back to what I was saying about me looking forward to moving to West-London to stay with my friend, 'K' and her daughter.

All I kept thinking to myself is

"I am moving from lonely to homely"

Taking time out from being by myself to now staying at my friends for a while, until I got myself sorted. Though if truth be known for all those who knew both of us and heard I was leaving south were telling me that I was making a mistake due to her being a woman of drama, though they weren't telling me anything I did not already know. But for me, I respected and accepted her ways from back-in-the-day, she did not have much if any self-respect, a little lost within herself and known as trashy and easy by some, both boys and girls, yet she 'kept it real' (well) so I thought!

K was someone from my secondary school days. We hung about in a big group together, but she was not one of my tight (close) friends. Though I respected her ways, I was not feeling being too associated with her because she was always in beef (trouble) from girls to boys wanting to fight her, to sleeping around and having no respect for herself. But that was back then in the 9Ts we were now both grown, one a single mother and the other me a single lady finally putting myself first.

We had grown closer over the past few years, so when she heard, I was looking to move (again) this time away from South-East London. Which is when she suggested I relocate up to West London and I could not wait! Never did I expect by eight-weeks and 3days of me moving in with her in Shepherds Bush to then embark on something you see in the movies.

The biggest, unexpected, and shocking experience in my life to date which I will never forget! Bearing in mind, a few people tried to warn me off moving in with her as they knew that drama followed always, but I thought that she had changed for the better due to now being a mum to her beautiful daughter. Boi, all I can say is.

> *"You don't know someone until you live with them or go on holiday."*

Is a fact and what happened next is living proof! I was the newbie to the area and people knew it as they would say.

> *"I knew you weren't a West-Londoner or from the endz"*

Literally, from May' 2011, these are the times when Christian first took me under his wing, wherever he was there I was too, he'd come by K's flat to see us, then two-twos we'd be back on the road like **'Batty and Bench'** having pure laughter. If we were not in Bush (Shepherds Bush), we would be out and about in either Hammersmith, Notting Hill, Westend and on his own born and grown endz of Ladbroke Grove. Whenever he was out at a party, event, or his top favourite invite which I have attended too many times, funeral receptions. The git would always manage to get me to go with him as I knew I was always guaranteed to have good times and great vibes wherever I was out and about with Christian. He has stories galore that he has shared with me from his life growing up in West London, mixing and personally knowing some well-known celebrities. Wherever there is people, music, food, and drink that is where you will find him, this man loves to make people laugh, smile, and always wants to make everyone happy, including me!

Though he'd say I can be a miserable bitch at times or too hard and cold, he loves me all the same and visa-versa as no matter how much he upsets me or is unreliable, I know that he is a good man and what you see is what you get 'The Real Deal'. I remember once during many conversations he said to me.

CHRISTIAN: *"You bring me luck."*

ME: *"Why do you think I bring you luck."*

CHRISTIAN: *"Not all the time, but people who don't believe in God think its luck but its destined, it is already been written. In fact, you don't bring me luck; you build my persona."*

ME: *"Aww, that's a beautiful thing to say."*

CHRISTIAN: *"Yerrrr, that's why I don't like you"* (we both laughed)

I have nothing but love and respect for him and miss the Biatch when he 'ghosts' me for months on end. You cannot go out with him and not have a good time, but after a while, the funeral reception invites were becoming too regular. Though I wanted to support him, I started feeling uncomfortable at attending (if I did not know them) so stopped going as it just did not feel right!

But for the few that I did attend with him out of support, company and because there would be one or two people that would be there that I knew through Christian like his brother Johnny or his close friend Cheda'rins! Plus, I knew he loved having me by his side and I enjoyed being out and about with him too. He enjoyed the attention from associates and people who had not spoken to him in ages. Some guys even offering to buy him drinks and he would say to them.

"I know you've only come over to speak to me, hoping that I'll introduce you to my friend."

Then once they had gone, we would start laughing! People found it hard to believe that we were just friends and never had anything more. A couple of weeks of me living in Shepherds Bush, he offered to take me swimming so that he could see my body, Lol! Christian is a handsome, good looking, gentleman, with one or two turn-offs (his teeth) being the main dislike but apart from that, I know any female would be lucky to have him as their man or husband as he is a good man who always carried my shopping bags or even my handbag at times. He is a lover of massaging feet which I had the pleasure of enjoying mostly in the first year or two of me living in West-London.

I know from him telling me this and sharing stories about how much he loves to **EATTT** (his words) LMFAO!!!

Will leave you (the reader) to use your imagination and no in case you are wondering he has not had the pleasure of mine, wishful thinking in his dreams! Could we have been more than friends, I do not know as I have never looked at him romantically and not being able to see past his mouth is something I could never consider. Regardless I accept him for who he is, he will always be my Bestie and would not change him, or his challenging ways which makes me so mad at times but that is him and it is what it is! x

Tuesday, 28th June 2011, while at work. I received a call from Christian (who became my rock) through the 'aftermath' of this incident. He called to let me know that the police had arrested 'K' and he had both her daughter as well as my friend Elenore's daughter. What the hell was my first thought, followed by how and why? El, who I met back in '2010 during our training at the <u>Identity Drama School</u> in Dalston called me screaming in hysterics and crying down the phone asking me

"Where is my child"

Having left her in the care of 'K' for the day. I reassured her not to worry as she was with Christian safe and sound. Thank God! Can you believe that he nearly went with 'K' in the cab for the ride as he had nothing doing. It was only due to one of his grandchildren pleading with him to stay with them, as to why he did not go with her! OMG, the **'what if'** is unthinkable!

I was working down at Moorgate on the Heron project, a new contracted job that I had only been working at for a few weeks. I left work straight away to head home and nothing could prepare me for what I was about to walk into and see. The whole flat had been turned upside down by the police, but what the fuck were they searching for is what I wanted to know?! You name it nothing had been left untouched, including my things too. They had taken my passport and driving license, WTF!

None of what was going on or taken place had anything to do with me, but here I was smack in the middle of what I did not know! What had this girl gone and done having only got back a few days from holiday and now she has been arrested and here I was fresh in West London left to pick up the pieces, get her home back in order, while unsure whether more police would be coming to knock at the door! Once I had got my head around the state of the flat and 'K' being arrested I made my way into the living room and all the answers to my questions had been left via this note (below) which was left on top of the TV by the police which said.

ARREST

On Tuesday 28th June 2011 at approximately 11:57hrs ! was seen to park his grey VW Polo ____, W14. He then got out of his vehicle and walked towards _____ in, W14. At approximately 12:03hrs officers saw ! meet with ! in ____, W14, where he was seen to place a parcel into a Tesco's bag which ! was carrying. Both ! and ! then parted and at this point, the car was stopped and detained by officers. ! was seen to get into the rear of the red car parked in ____, W14.

The vehicle was stopped, and ! was also detained. A search of the car was carried out and found on the back seat next to where ! was sitting was the Tesco's carrier bag she had been seen carrying. Upon searching the bag, it was found to contain a brown taped parcel wrapped in white tissue paper which was the same parcel that had been placed into the bag by !. This was later confirmed to be half a kilo of Heroin at 32% Purity.

At 12:05hrs ! was arrested for possession of a controlled drug and intent to supply. He made no reply to caution. At 12:05hrs ! was arrested for conspiracy to supply a controlled drug. Upon caution, she replied, "I am just trying to make a living for my child and me it is hard out there, there are no jobs. I was just dropping something off for a friend". ! and ! were then conveyed to Notting Hill police station. A search of ! Conningham Road, W12, which was given as the Home address for ! revealed 38g of Crack Cocaine and Paraphernalia such as weighing scales. Miss ! pleaded guilty to the offence of possession with intent to supply, in regard to the Heroine and Crack Cocaine.

This is a true and accurate statement of events.

What can I say, except never in a million years did I expect to go through something like this! All I could think was the police must have been watching and surveillance 'K's' movements for months or years before deciding on that day to move in and make the arrest! I could have been behind bars, or what if I had been at home chilling, smoking a spliff, like I was before finding new contracted work. To then have the shock of the police breaking down the door, coming to do a raid and me thinking I am in a nightmare wondering what the hell is going on! **What if** she had stashed her 'A' class drugs in the living room, where I slept who knows what the fuck could have happened to me. All I know is God and my guardian angels protected me that day like never before! Just like her young daughter, I too was an innocent party among this unexpected disaster. 'K' was lucky because she was given three years and served half. She did the crime and done time.

Unfortunately, though I understand that sometimes people do things that they do not want to out of desperation but at that point, I had lost all respect for her after this for a while. I remained living in her home; after all, I had nowhere else to go having been there for just over two months. I started paying the rent while also trying to pay off the serious arrears that she had accumulated hoping I could remain there, so she would still have her flat once released. How wrong was I!

The council found out what had happened with 'K' being arrested and sent to prison; therefore, they wanted to repossess the flat, so I was on the verge of being homeless and out of work due to my contracted job at The Heron project coming to an end. I was in shock, worried and scared for a good while in disbelief at what had taken place, how was I now back by myself living at 'K's who was now in prison for drugs.

What if the owner of the drugs, came to the flat looking for payment or answers, what if they were watching me, how could I be sure that I was safe? The simple fact is I did not know shit! All I could do was hope and pray for God to keep me safe and to not let this *'out of my hands'* drama send me overboard as I honestly did not know how much more I could take! But I can confess at one point I felt like I reached the edge of a nervous breakdown, having seen myself in the state of shock. This build up was the delayed reaction of all that had happened a few months after the event took place in June. 'K' was now out on 'tag' staying by her Dads' back in Catford, down the road from where I moved from to join her in West London, how crazy is that!

Here is one (out of the eight) 'prison letter' received from her. Just like photos and footage memorabilia, I also have every letter ever written to me from people during my secondary school years. Plus, from those who ended up in prison and kept in contact by either writing letters or emails via the website email a prisoner which are all part of my life journey.

04/07/2011

Dear Niki

Hey babe, I got your letter this morning which made me cry!!! I miss you so much, just those little things. You asked if I need anything well a book for me to write my diary, I deffo want one right now.

'S' brought a load of rubbish, I need proper clothes PJ's, underwear, shoes some slippers socks. Also, with the money I get can you pay 'V' every 1st of the month for my phone bill, please. Did you find my card, hope you have? I need your phone number you did not put it in the letter. I have to book your visit and then the prison will let you know the day and time, so let me know what day you guys are coming. Tell 'V' to put her numbers in the letter she sends so I can call her thanks.

If you are going to send me both Martina Cole, is my author!!! I cannot call anyone until next week as my money will not drop until Friday, no canteen for me this week so sorry babe. I miss 'S' Nik; I am finding it hard to get on in here without even seeing her. I want to see her smile, hear her voice, hear her cry. I woke up at 06:30 today as I would have been taken her to nursery. I am praying to God to have mercy on me for my sentence, I am thinking 5years, but anything less is a bonus.
Miss ya. K

I would say her prayer worked and thank God her time served was not that long so that it would not impact on her daughter's life because she was still young only five so hopefully won't remember too much of her mums' absence. So, before she knew it, she was out and back doing what she was prior taking care of her child. It was the first time that we would be meeting up on an evening out, having invited her for drinks with my work colleagues and me. It was great to have her company, but her time was limited so when she had to leave, I set off too and it was not until we got to the tube station that everything hit me. We weren't going home together, she was going back to our old endz Catford and I was going to hers in Shepherds Bush, we hugged, and I can't remember if I broke down crying as we were separating or as I was making my way to the tube!

What I do know is I was in floods of tears on the tube with people watching me, still crying as I walked up the road home just inconsolable. Christian came around; he could not believe his eyes, having never seen me like that before, I was bawling uncontrollably. I hope never to experience anything like this again. Looking back on this and researching the delayed reaction, I think this may have been what I experienced,

Delayed-Onset PTSD.' Post-Traumatic Stress Disorder, *Delayed-onset PTSD describes a situation where a person does not develop a PTSD diagnosis until at least six months after a traumatic event.*

2011, was undoubtedly a year that I thought would be the start of something new and great having moved away from family stress and drama. To going through an unexpected, traumatic experience only a few wks. after moving to West-London to start afresh! Why was my life filled with so many tribulations what had I done to deserve this instead of happiness and contentment? Here's a page written in my diary on **Saturday 5th November '2011**, Titled.

FEEL TO JUST END IT ALL | PHONES OFF

Dear diary, once again, I am being challenged with a (knock to the system) that I have not experienced before. Out of all the times I

have been unemployed, I have never had to think about being unemployed and homeless too at the same time until now. Whereas before if I struggled for rent, I would borrow it from Nanny via mum or from housing benefit, but this is not the case anymore. I am living in West London in 'K's place which is in £300+ rent arrears; bailiffs want to come and take her things to clear a £400 debt. There is an outstanding council tax and EDF intends to come and turn off the electric as she owes them £600+ and I have NOTHING, no money and nowhere to go absolute Nish (nothing)!

All I want to do is sleep, dream and not wake-up to the reality of my lonely, sad, depressing, unemployed, semi-homeless life. Would I be missed if I were no longer here? Who would even find my body as I have no one in West London except Christian and I pissed him off to the point where he is not talking to me?

Then my Dad who lives one stop away but does not give two shits about me, knowing full well what has taken place but yet he is nowhere to be seen but thinks calling me (once in a blue moon) is worthy. I think I need to lock him off again because he is partly to blame for my angry, cold, bitter, and bitchy ways. I tried to stay strong, but the tears would not hold back, only God knows how I am feeling and how weak I am dealing with life like this on my own. But maybe I am a wicked bitch that deserves nothing but lows and unhappiness, but deep down inside I know that is not true. I am a decent person who is Important, Worthy and I will Succeed.

South-East London is where I was born and bred so it will always be the Best!

Through this (never want to experience again) traumatic time, I am happy that I got to get away later in the year to somewhere that I have always wanted to go, Los Angeles, for Networking and Pleasure having attended the **'Hollywood Black Film Festival'** in West Hollywood with a friend called Hannah who also attended Cator Park Girls Secondary

School. What a fantastic trip we had there together. Well done to us for going even though neither of us has made it back but we networked, went to the famous Hollywood Walk of Fame, and stayed in a superb hotel. It is most def a place I want to return to and would move out there if the opportunity or romance presented itself. It is Fabulous!

Thank you to my friend (IG: jbseriousfilms) who I met out there. He took me under his wing and introduced me to my first ever Stripper Club experience, could not have gone to watch in a more lavish place like the one he took me too. American's certainly do their things different! An incredible holiday with great memories, footage, and pics. Great memories, thank you JB.x

<u>2020</u>

It is now November and first and foremost, R.I.P to all during this pandemic! The beautiful PDA (public display of affection) photo below taken in July this year by me walking hand-in-hand with the man who declared he had fallen in love with me after three days of us talking. I believe we are Soulmates; the Love of my Life and he has asked me to be his wife! Here is a little of what I had written back on the 9th Sep dedicated to him my NbN.x

__Thank you Boo, my delicious simply for being you. Those big hands, the unconditional affection that you show me, how much you tell me you love me along with the hugs, kisses, and the rest. Lol! I cannot get enough of all of it. We make each other happy the same way we can make each other upset but no relationship is smooth sailing all the time plus we are still getting to know each other.__

__The other day I was on a downer at work, you came and surprised me to cheer me up, which meant so much! Never experienced that before, it was beautiful and you had me smiling from ear to ear, it is the small things that mean a lot and that certainly did, thank you. We have a__

strong love that has developed so quick I hope we have a long, bright, and happy future ahead. Amen.x

He is a manly man who is family orientated, creative, stubborn, helpful with a big heart and a no-filter (worse mouth) than mine though he would not agree, Lol! God does not give more than you can handle, we have certainly been challenged from the start in our relationship no regrets because I know.

"Nothing Worth Having Comes Easy"

No one knows what any relationship holds, let alone a new one so you can only go with your feelings, heart and how you both feel when together. Love, Respect and Trust is key though we are all guilty of our own insecurities. Only God knows how much I want to find 'the one' hope this is finally it as we both deserve to be happy and loved unconditionally!

I hope one if not both of my parents get to meet him too! Only time will tell, watch this space! Amen. #soulmates

Nothing will keep us apart if we are meant to be together. If not, this pic will be one memory that will always be special to me!

Plus, this gorgeous compliment that was said to us from an elderly woman... so true! #NoRegrets

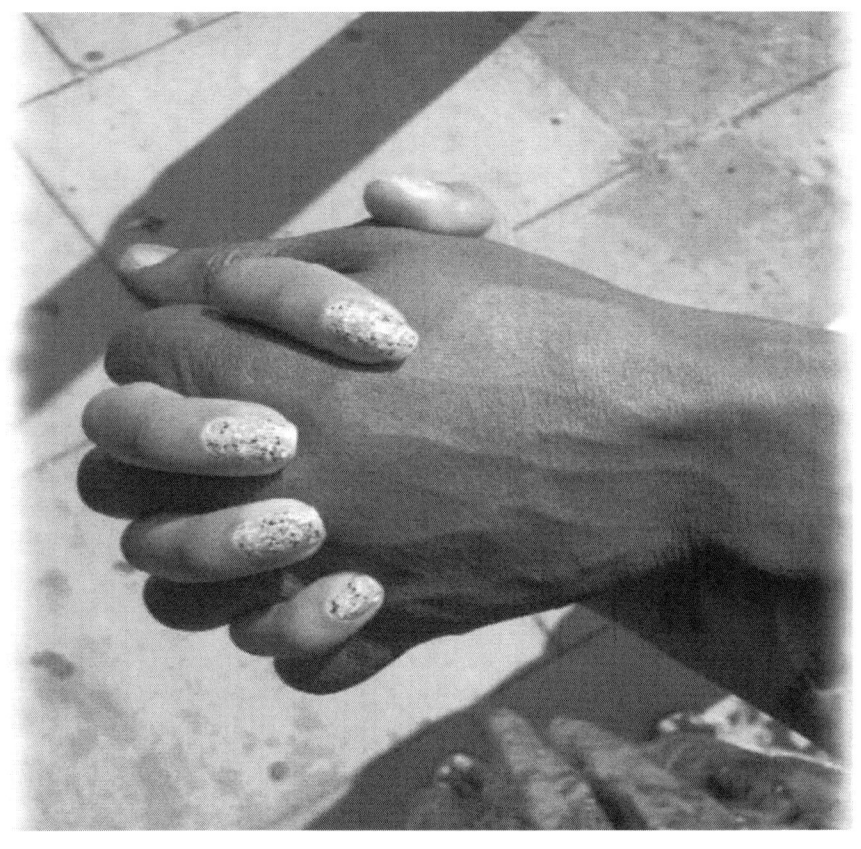

"Its Beautiful 2 C A Black Couple Holding Hands"

WE ALL LEARN LESSONS
IN LIFE SOME STICK,

SOME DON'T.
I HAVE ALWAYS LEARNED

MORE FROM
REJECTION AND FAILURE

THAN FROM
ACCEPTANCE AND SUCCESS

Henry Rollins

Hollywood Black Film Festival '2011

Roof-Top of West Hollywood Hotel '2011

THROWBACK PICS

From Birth to 2011-Onwards

Thank you for all the great memories

Shared in these photos!

Present or Not in my life

Love to you all.x

My Creators at my 30th Birthday Party '2011

Welcome to the world... Me!

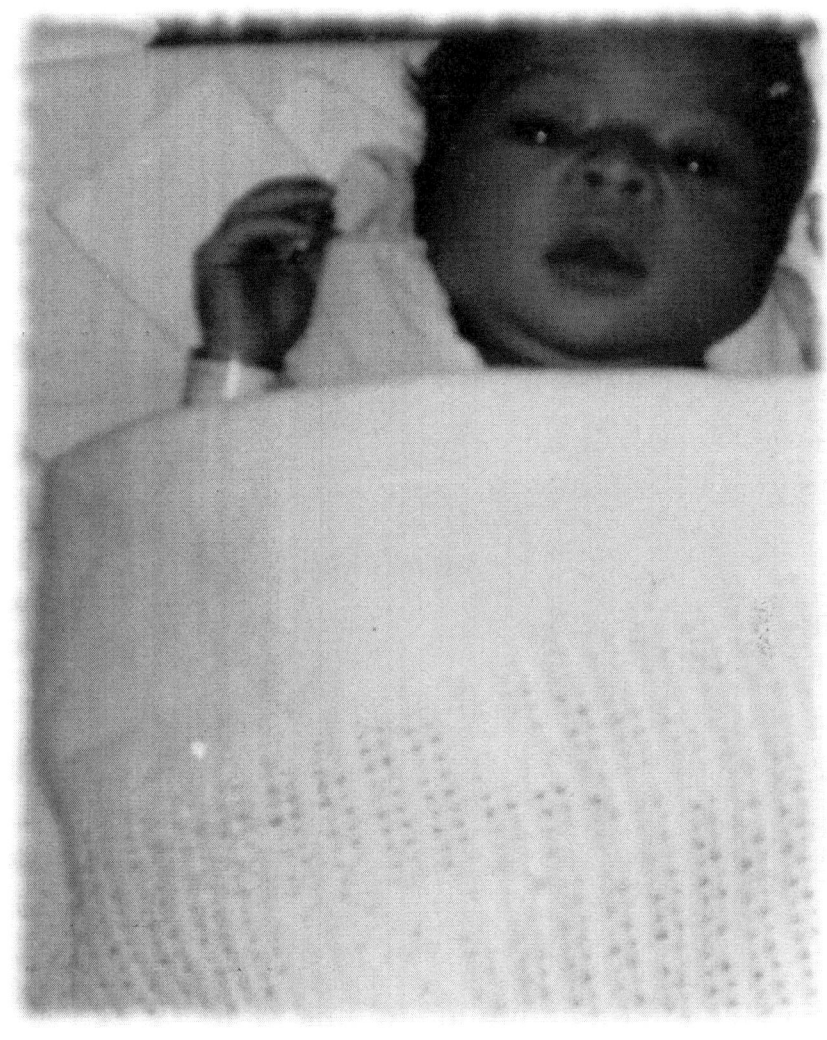

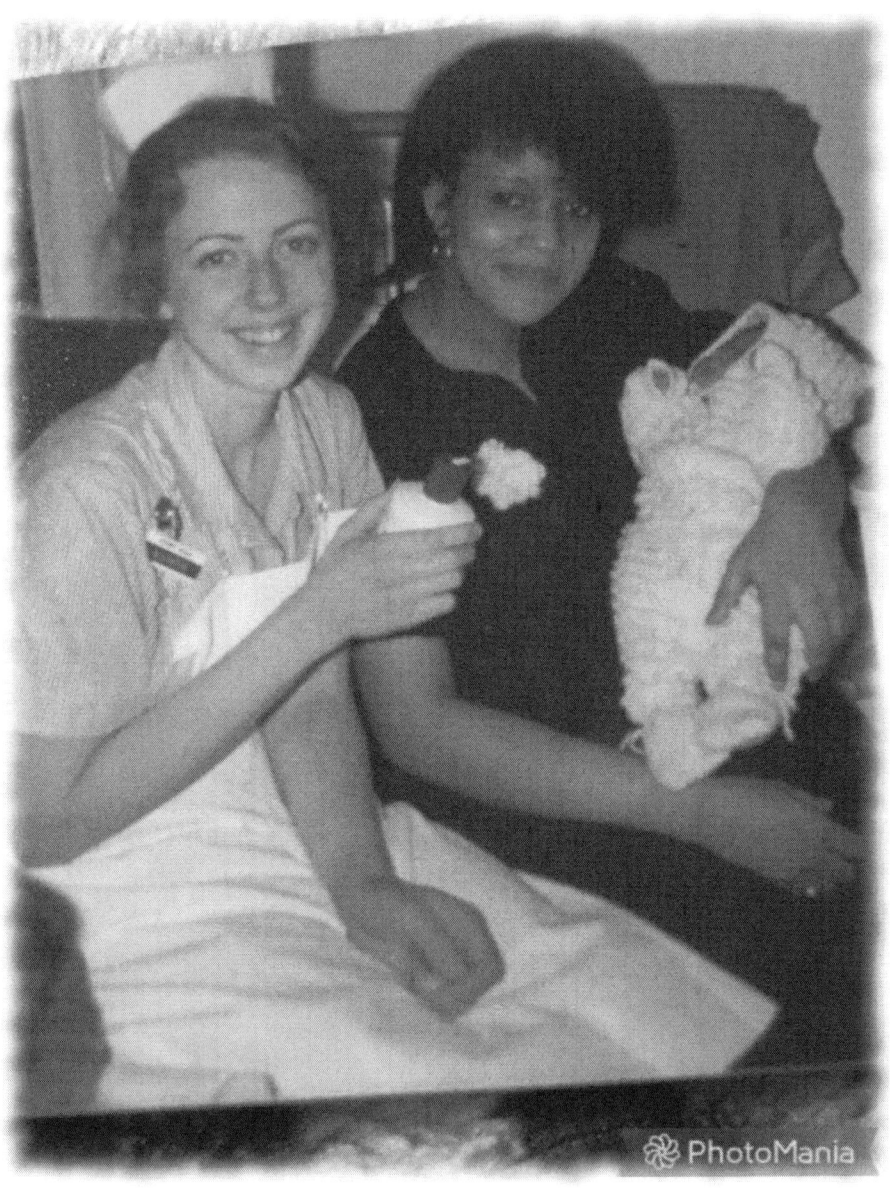

Not sure if this is the Nurse who passed out when I was born!

Sibling Love

Godfather

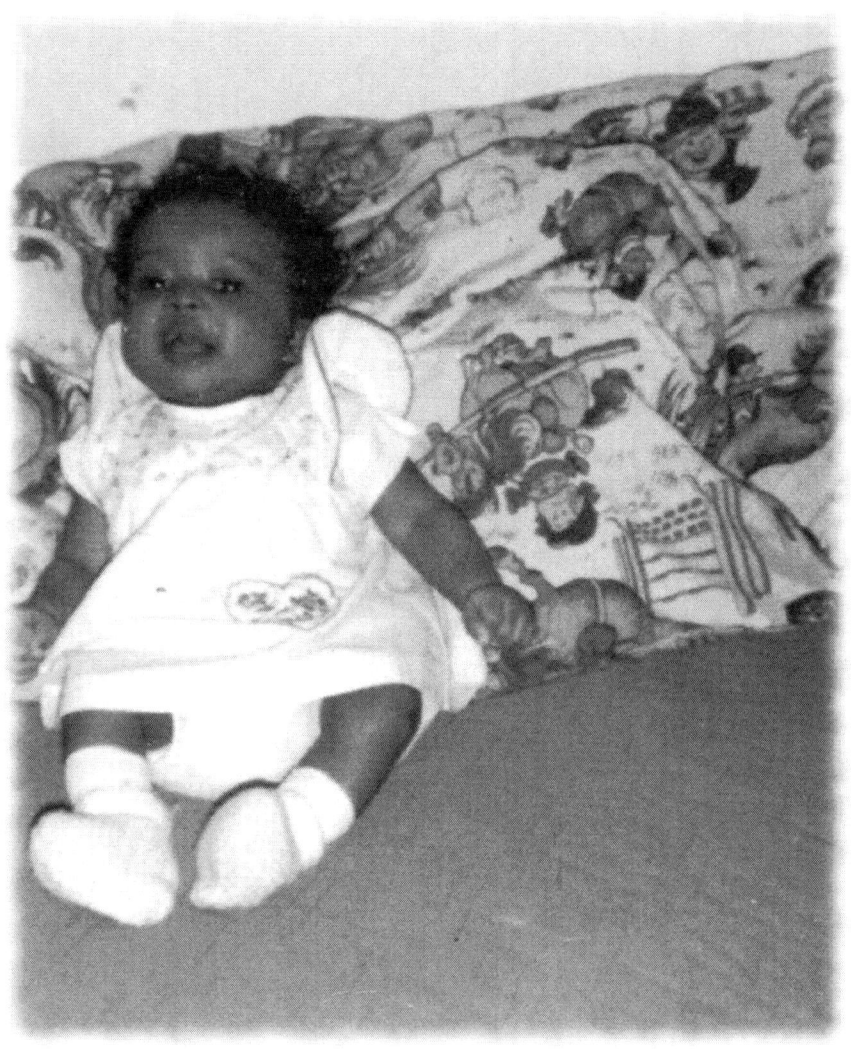

Mum, Bro and Likkle Me

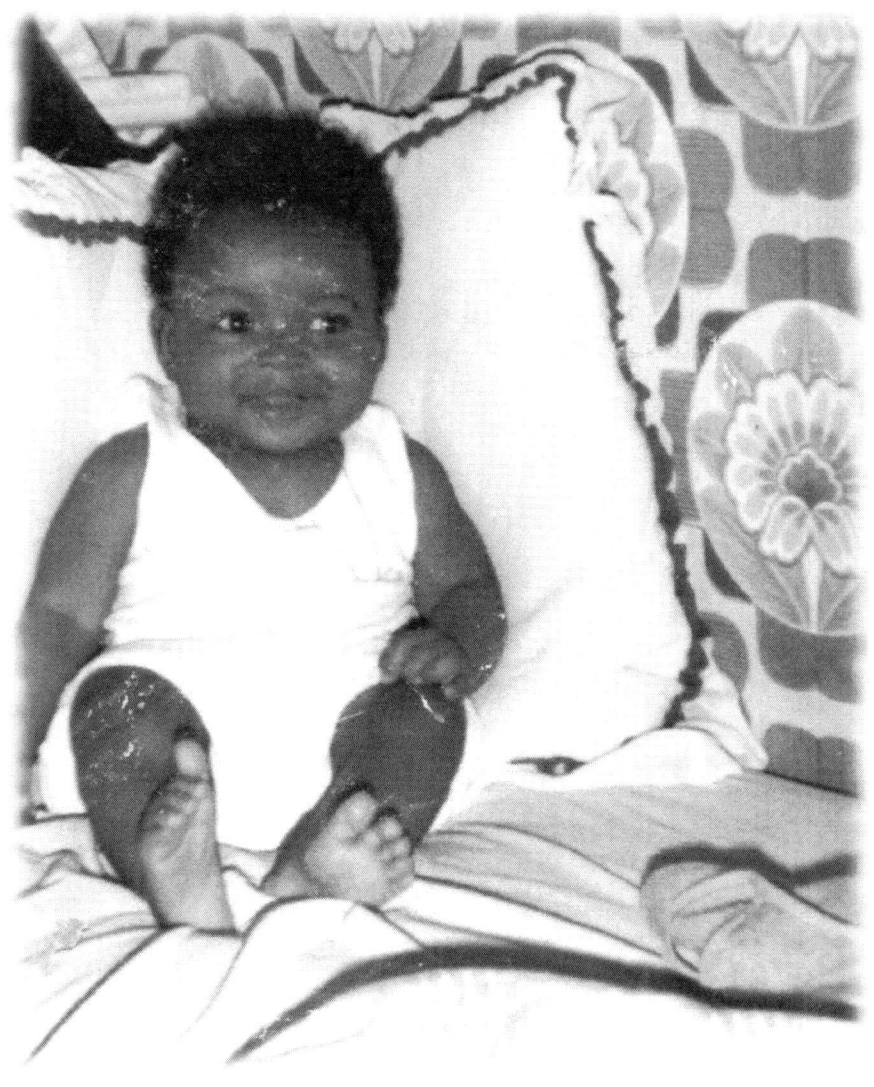

Mum and Me

Last Christmas Spent with Nan in the Nursing Home '2011

Smiley Culture (March for Justice) '2011

Christian (Bessie-mate) and Me '2015/16

'2020

'2015

'2019

Original Book Cover Photo '2016

Printed in Great Britain
by Amazon